ACT ONE
EVERYTHING AND THE KITCHEN SINK

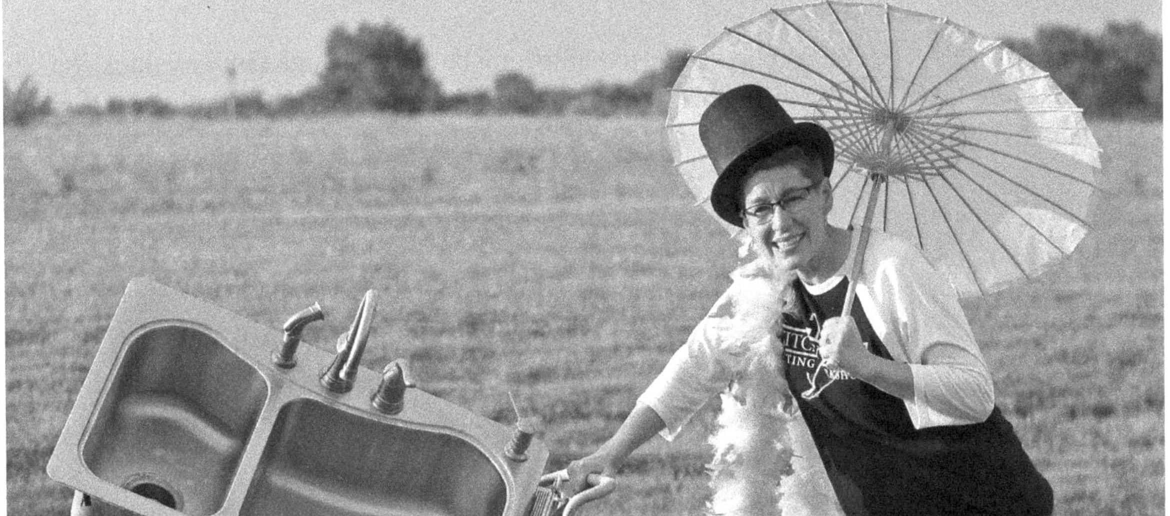

CHERYL L. WESTON

ACT ONE

Everything and the Kitchen Sink

Copyright © 2017
By Cheryl L Weston

Published by 21st Century Press
Springfield, MO 65807

21st Century Press is a publisher dedicated to publishing books with high family values. We believe the vision for 21st Century Press is to provide families and individuals with user-friendly materials that will help them in their daily lives and experiences.

It is our hope that this book will help you discover truths for your own life and help you meet the needs of others. May you be richly blessed.

All rights reserved. No part of this book may be used or reproduced in any manner whatsoever or stored in any database or retrieval system without written permission except in the case of brief quotations used in critical articles and reviews. Requests for permissions should be addressed to:

21st Century Press
2131 W. Republic Rd. PMB 211
Springfield, MO 65807
417-889-4803
email: lee@21stcenturypress.com
www.21stcenturypress.com

Book and Cover Design: Lee Fredrickson

ISBN: 978-0-9981392-5-8

Printed in the United States of America

DEDICATION

To my dear friend, Jalinn, who once asked the question,
"Will you teach me how to act?"

KITCHEN SINK
ACTING WORKSHOP

Welcome to the Kitchen Sink. Pull up a sponge. If you are afraid of dishpan hands, then feel free to slip on a pair of yellow rubber gloves. But be prepared to take the plunge into the sometimes clear, and yet, often murky world of acting.

Contents

DEDICATION 3

Introduction 7

Relaxation 11

Sight 15

Hearing 21

Smell and Taste - Part One 27

Smell and Taste - Part Two 31

Touch 37

Spirit 43

Observation 49

Improvisation 55

Blocking and Movement 59

Voice - Part One 67

Voice - Part Two 75

Animal Instincts 87

Audition Tips 91

ACT ONE

Why Choose An Acting Technique

Introduction

As a beginning actor, finding a favorite acting style can be hard and a bit confusing. Why? Because there are so many acting techniques from which to choose. Knowing which style is a fit for you can be like "looking for a needle in a haystack." For the purposes of this class, I will introduce you to four of the most famous methods and their creators: Konstantin Stanislavski, Lee Strasberg, Stella Adler and Sanford Meisner. And I will tell you about one style that has remained unknown, until now.

Why is it important to choose an acting style or technique?
_____
_____
_____

FIVE FAMOUS METHODS

Konstantin Stanislavski (1863-1963) was a Russian director and actor. To this day, he is one of the most influential figures in American theatre. The name for his acting technique is called the Stanislavski system, and the most popular part of his system is "the method." This style asks, "What would I do if I were in the character's situation?" Basically, if whatever circumstances of the scene were happening to you, how would you react? What would you do? Why would you do it? Objectives should be based on actions the character can physically achieve, rather than some "internal" goal. This way, you can produce action onstage that the audience can see, rather than acting it all out in the mind. He advised actors to recall different emotional experiences they have had in the past. For example, if your character has just lost their grandfather, recall your own personal experience with a death in the family.

Lee Strasberg (1901-1982), an American actor, acting teacher, and director, was a strong supporter of method acting. He had an interest in psychology, which was quite influential in his acting techniques. He advised actors to dive fully into researching every aspect of his or her character, especially their backstory and personal life before the story begins. One of his goals was to

ACT ONE

have actors become so familiar with their characters' lives that the characters would be just as real as the actors' own lives. Memory was also important to Strasberg. He asked actors to try and remember as many reactions, thoughts, and feelings as possible through everyday living and try to apply them to a character going through the same experiences.

Stella Adler (1901-1992) was an American actress who founded two famous schools of acting in New York and Los Angeles. Stella believed in many of Stanislavski's teachings, but she also stressed the importance of being big, and not boring, onstage. Small and subtle movements? No. Unlike some teachers who supported very little preparation for the sake of spontaneity, Adler encouraged a lot of it. She wanted actors to rehearse often, taking in the minor details more and more each time. Submerging oneself in the environment, the character, and the situation was her lesson. Adler's technique can be better adapted toward monologues or cold readings where the scene partner may be the director and not a fellow actor.

Sanford Meisner (1905-1997) was an American actor who developed what is now known as the Meisner technique. A form of method acting, his technique emphasizes the importance of finding a motivation for every moment, whether it is silence, dialogue, or action. Like Stanislavski, he stressed always having a real goal for the character, rather than just "feeling it." His technique is where the "live truthfully under fictional circumstances" comes into play. He did not want actors to merely play the emotion in the script; he wanted the subtext of the lines and the emotions of the goals to guide the actor into their next moment. Another technique Meisner was known for was memorizing lines without vocal inflections or gestures. The technique says that by having actors learn their lines "dry," the actual delivery onstage will be more natural instead of pre-prepared. He embraced spontaneity; not knowing what will happen until the moment occurs onstage.

ONE "NOT SO FAMOUS" METHOD

Cheryl Weston (1968) is an amateur actress and life-long Speech and Theatre Education major at Missouri State University. Her early acting experiences were influenced solely by the Stanislavski technique of method acting with a dash of Stella Adler thrown in for good measure. While she still relies on those acting principles from time to time today, Cheryl realized that she had developed her own style of acting over the years, a style that

Introduction

she fondly calls "The Kitchen Sink." She found that she depends more on her five senses to trigger certain emotional memories in her own psyche. Simply stated, "sense memory" is the uncanny ability to store certain impressions, experienced in everyday life, by way of the five senses. These impressions are stored in the subconscious. The actor can learn to recall these sensory impressions from the subconscious by concentrating on the stimuli associated with them.

Have you ever been so hungry that the tiniest thought of your favorite food caused your mouth to water? This stimuli recall is an example of your taste buds responding to the memory of the food. Have you ever reached into a darkened closet to grab your favorite sweater just by touching it alone? Your sense of touch "remembered" the unique feeling of its fabric against your skin. Training actors to become more aware of their five senses – sight, hearing, touch, taste, and smell – can make them even more aware of their surroundings and the emotions that follow. As far back as the 1760's, the famous philosopher Immanuel Kant proposed that our knowledge of the outside world depends on our modes of perception. Our worldview. Yes. It is important to know what your character wants and why. But the imaginary scent of musky rain in the air or the itchy sensation of dry earth underfoot can do so much to enrich a character's believability. It will allow the actor to shine past the mythical fourth wall with brilliance and integrity. And for good measure, Cheryl has thrown in a 6th sense, the spirit. And honestly, this should be the highest of all the senses. "The spirit of man is the lamp of the Lord, searching all his innermost parts" (Proverbs 20:27).

Exercise One:

Choose a monologue that you feel will challenge you or choose one that is within your comfort zone. I would prefer that you challenge yourself. Read over it. Make sure you are happy with your choice.

Monologue Title: _____

Written by: _____

Character name: _____ Estimated Age of Character: _____

ACT ONE

You will each take turns reading your selection aloud. This is called a "cold reading." It is normal to feel a bit timid and nervous during a cold reading, especially if your reading skills are not very good. But it is okay. Take your time, if you need to. There is no hurry.

Write down comments or thoughts that your fellow students will share with you about your selection and the character itself. Their ideas might help you later. Fill out a character sheet located at the back of this book.

_____
_____
_____
_____
_____
_____
_____

This is the monologue that you will perform for your final examination at the close of your semester.

Lesson One

Relaxation

Before the actor begins any training, rehearsal or performance, they should always engage in some relaxation exercise to clear themselves physically, mentally, and emotionally. Performers, who are tense, tend to look tense, over-anticipate things and make poor acting choices with their movements. Until an actor is properly relaxed onstage, they cannot convey the thoughts and emotions which move their character through the events of the play. Instead, the audience will see a frightened actor and not a believable character. Relaxation is also recommended before any sensory exercise, which involves reliving a sensation, like a smell or a sight or a sound. These recreated sensations can trigger certain emotions within the actor that might be beneficial when creating a character within a scene.

Name some types of tension that you might experience.
1. _____
2. _____
3. _____
4. _____

Everyone gets nervous before a rehearsal or performance, no matter how big or how small. Some actors reduce their tension by listening to music, doing a few yoga stances or vocal warm ups. A friend of mine prefers to sit in a chair, snacking on a cookie or a bag of M&M's while enjoying the quietness of the space around him. A few brave actors choose to embrace their jitters and channel all that built-up energy into their performances. Not me. I prefer to pray, having a little conversation with God, and run through a series of breathing exercises. You will eventually develop your own routine for relaxation.

Until you do, we will perform one of the following relaxation exercises at the beginning of class, as time allows, that will help you to identify specific areas of tension within yourself. Only after proper relaxation will you be ready to concentrate on your character and the rehearsal at hand. It is also important to warm-up before a performance.

ACT ONE

Exercise One:

1. Remove your shoes and any heavy articles of clothing like jackets or coats.
2. Lie down on the floor with your back to the ground.
3. Raise your knees to a comfortable position, making sure your feet and knees are parallel.
4. Lay your arms comfortably to your sides or your hands resting gently on your stomach.
5. Listen to some soothing music or sound effects of nature, and visualize yourself somewhere peaceful. Remember the images that come to mind. Put yourself there.
6. Starting with the soles of your feet, slowly imagine each part of your body melting down into the floor as you move toward your head. Acknowledge any tension that you feel and make a concentrated effort to release that tension.
7. Take your time. If you are working on your arms and suddenly notice renewed tension in your calves, stop to remind the legs muscles to melt away. Then resume the work on your arms.
8. Work to relax all the way to the top of your head. The goal is to become a puddle of mush.
9. Breathe. Nice, slow and relaxed breathing from your diaphragm.
10. The goal is to recognize tension when you feel it and equip yourself with the knowledge to get rid of that tension.

Exercise Two:

1. Stand with your arms at your sides, with both feet shoulder width apart.
2. Stretch your right arm up. Stretch your left arm up. Slowly lower your arms together. Repeat.
3. Roll your head to the front, right, back, and left. Repeat.
4. Roll your shoulders to the front, up, back, and down. Repeat.
5. Bend from your waist forward, to the right, back, and left. Repeat.
6. Step forward with your right foot (leaving your left foot in place). Stretch. Switch, step forward with your left foot (leaving your right foot in place). Stretch. Repeat.
7. Shake out your hands, your head, and shoulders, your legs and feet. Shake out your whole body.

Relaxation

8. Stand quietly with your arms at your sides.

9. Breathe in to the count of 1,2,3,4. Breathe out to the count of 1,2,3,4. Repeat.

What are some ways that you might be able to relax before a rehearsal or performance?

1. _____
2. _____
3. _____
4. _____
5. _____
6. _____

Homework Assignment One:

Complete the chart on the next page over the course of this week. Set aside one day a week to perform these relaxation exercises. Find some music that you consider to be "relaxing." Spotify, Pandora, and even some sound machine apps are a great place to start your search. It will be a graded assignment.

ACT ONE

Relaxation Chart	Length of Time								
	Date								
	Type								

Lesson Two

Sight

The old saying, "a picture is worth a thousand words" is true in the world of theatre. The ability to remember certain images in your mind is important to creating and sustaining a make-believe world on the stage. The stronger and clearer those images become for you, the actor, the easier it will be to believe the dialogue in the script and relate to the character you are portraying. To truly become a new character, you must see what is around that character. And even on them. Search out visually stimulating words in the script. Highlight them, if necessary. Analyze them. Then proceed to find the matching images within your own memory vault and take advantage of the emotions they arouse. Use those emotions to improve your personal interpretation of the story, setting or character.

Exercise One:
Listen as your teacher reads the following excerpt from Lindsey Gonzales' sketch, "Writing Matthew's Gospel." If a word from Lindsey's sketch creates a visual image in your mind, circle it. Then write the associated memory or emotion it created on the lines provided afterwards.

How could I forget? I can still smell the air, it was cool and crisp, fresh coming from the sea! Matthew, it was the most beautiful place Jesus could have picked. It was like the whole mountain was made just for that moment! The flowers were in bloom. They were pink, red and white surrounding the open space we were sitting in. There were trees that enclosed the area giving us plenty of shade. I remember being so thankful for the trees because it was so hot with all of us packed together. Jesus stood at the front of the crowd while the rest of us sat and listened. It was amazing. Behind Him we could see the mountains and the sea of Galilee. It was peaceful that day and quiet. In fact, we could hear everything He said. It was the perfect place to tell us something that was so important.

ACT ONE

_____
_____
_____
_____
_____

Take time to share your images with the group.

Exercise Two:

Look at the following pictures. Write the first word or adjective that pops into your mind directly below it. Be prepared to explain why.

SIGHT

Exercise Three:

List the first five geographical locations that pop into your mind. It can be a spot at the bottom of the Grand Canyon or on the surface of the moon. Or even be in this very room.

1. _____
2. _____
3. _____
4. _____
5. _____

Think about these locations for a few minutes. What would you see at these places? Use your imagination to look all around you. Look up. Look down. Look all around you, and narrow your choice down to one location. Record what you might see there.

_____
_____
_____

As a group, take turns sharing one of your locations, taking the rest of us on a virtual tour by using your words, both adjectives and nouns, to describe what you see. Get creative!

Homework Assignment Two:

Choose one of the images below. Write a short story, no more than five minutes long, about the image you have chosen. Make up character names and character histories. What do the characters want? What might be some obstacles to their desires? Based on what you see, use that image to create a colorful tapestry for an intriguing story.

Record your story on the next page. You will share your story at the next class. It will be a graded assignment.

ACT ONE

SIGHT

Application #1

What is the setting of your monologue?

_____

Stand in the middle of that setting, and look around. Take a virtual tour of the space around your character. Write down what you see in front of you, to your left, to your right, above you and at your feet. Do not forget to include a description of yourself. Are your hands gnarled with age or well-manicured? Do you have warts or long eyebrow hairs? What about orthodontia? I realize these are odd questions, but roll with it and let your imagination run wild.

_____
_____
_____
_____
_____
_____
_____
_____
_____
_____
_____
_____

Could the images you described above have any emotional impact on your character? If so, what?

_____
_____
_____
_____

ACT ONE

Improve Your Listening Skills

Lesson Three

Hearing

Why is hearing so important for good acting? Before we answer that question, we first need to discuss the difference between hearing and listening. Do you know the difference? If so, write it below.

_____
_____
_____
_____

Hearing is the act of receiving sound by way of the auditory canal. If you have a pair of working ears, hearing simply happens. It is an activity that you cannot control unless you own a pair of good ear plugs. Listening, on the other hand, is something that you must choose to do. It requires concentration so that your brain correctly processes the meanings of words or sentences that you hear, either obvious or hidden. So, our original question should really be, "Why is listening so important for good acting?"

LISTENING

Listening, or active listening can strengthen your performance by making you aware of the tone in your fellow actor's voices. That awareness will allow you to respond more naturally, not artificially. Do not pretend to listen to the other actors on the stage and then spit your lines out in return like a mindless computer. You would be basing your performance on memorization alone, which will create a one-dimensional character. Take time to "process" and fully absorb everything you hear to respond in an organic, real way. Listen and pay attention! Listen to the dialogue as though you have never heard those words spoken before. If you can master this, your performances will never be the same.

ACT ONE

Exercise One:

Your teacher will assign certain movements to the words: blue, button and boy. It can be as simple as jumping once, clapping twice, stepping to the right or stepping to the left. Your teacher will then read the following story aloud. As the students hear the chosen words, you must correctly perform the corresponding movement for that word or you will be out of the game. The last person standing wins.

Once upon a time, there was a little **boy** named Benjamin **Blue**. Benjamin **Blue** had the biggest **blue** eyes and the cutest **button** nose. And kind? Benjamin **Blue** was the kindest **boy** in all of **Button** Town. One day, he came home from the **Button** Town School for **Boys** with a very sad face. His mother, Mrs. **Blue**, asked, "Dear **boy**, why are you so **blue**?" Benjamin replied through big, **blue** tears, "I lost a **button** off me trousers today." And sure enough, there, on his little **boy** trousers, a **blue button** was missing. Mrs. **Blue** smiled and knew exactly what to do. "Don't be **blue**, my little **boy**," she said. She reached into her big **button** jar that sat on the blue shelf and pulled out a bright yellow **button**. "Oh, **boy**!" exclaimed Benjamin. "A yellow **button**? Me thinks I'll have the fanciest **boy** trousers in all of **Button** Town now!"

Was this easy? _____ Yes _____ No
Why?_____
_____

Before we move to the next exercise, it is important to define the meaning of tone in the human voice.

Tone is not what a person says, but how they say it. It indicates the difference between knowing to take the trash out now or in a few hours. It says everything. Tone, in my opinion, is basically composed of the following characteristics:

- Inflection
- Placement
- Garnish
- Accent

We will save the gorier details of tone for Lesson Twelve, Voice Part Two. For now, concentrate on becoming more aware of what you hear. Do not just listen to what people say, but how they say it. Realize that there is more than one way to say a word or phrase, and much more ways to respond to it.

Hearing

Exercise Two:

Listen to the words, "take out the trash" as your teacher repeats them. The objective is to make you take out the trash. Notice that the meaning of the sentence changes each time the actor changes the tone in their voice.

Match the phrase to its corresponding emotion.

1. _____   A. Anger

2. _____   B. Sadness

3. _____   C. Joy

4. _____   D. Fear

5. _____   E. Apathy

What were the vocal cues that gave each emotion away?

Sadness_____
_____
_____

Joy_____
_____
_____

Fear_____
_____
_____

Anger_____
_____
_____

Apathy_____
_____
_____

ACT ONE

Improvisational games are a great tool for perfecting active listening and proper response. You must listen to your fellow actors. Otherwise, you will miss an important cue or the opportunity to expand a creative idea. An improvisational scene will die if you are not actively listening to each other.

Exercise Three:

Find a partner. You will each be handed a hat. You will play a stereotypical character based upon the hat you wear (for example, an Englishman for a derby and a Ranch-hand for a cowboy hat). Sitting side by side, you each will take turns beginning a conversation that should follow the example below:

Actor One: Did you know?
Actor Two: Did I know what?
Actor One: Did you know that monkeys live in trees?

Allow a conversation to develop, based on that specific question, by listening to each other. When that conversation dies down, start a new one with another, "Did you know?"

Write down your thoughts on this exercise. What, if anything, did you learn from it?

_____
_____
_____
_____

HEARING

It is important to note that without hearing, active listening could never occur. So, it is only fair to give the sensory recall of hearing a moment in the spotlight too. The simple task of hearing, receiving and processing sound waves, can also be beneficial to an actor through the processes of tuning out and tuning in.

Tuning out

Distractions in the audience occur all the time during a performance. A cell phone rings. A baby cries. Someone has a coughing fit. I guaranty, it will happen. And as those annoying sound waves hit your eardrums, they will seek to destroy the illusion of reality that you and your fellow actors have worked so hard to achieve on the stage. What is your defense against these constant attacks? Stay focused. Keep your attention on the events occurring on the stage, unless of course, a true emergency arises like a fire, a tornado or an active shooter. If that is the case, then swiftly exit and do not look back. But if it is just an annoying man on the front row who cannot keep his voice down or a child loudly ripping into a candy wrapper, then

Hearing

quickly tune these background noises out. Tune them out by tuning into your character and the situation playing out on the stage.

Tuning In

What do I mean by "tuning in"? Remember the lesson on sight? Just as you create a virtual environment with your eyes, so should you create a virtual environment with your ears. Determine, in your mind, what sounds your character might hear at that given moment of their life, based on what you have heard in the past.

Exercise Four:

Write down what you might hear if you were in one of these environments, and then share your answers with the class.

Library_____
_____
_____

Circus_____
_____
_____

Ocean_____
_____
_____

War zone_____
_____
_____

Homework Assignment Three:

Another great exercise for active listening is a pantomime. Pantomime is a dramatic performance in which performers express feelings and actions through nonverbal gestures, usually set to music. Choose a song. It must be instrumental only, with no words, and it needs to be no longer than 3 – 4 minutes. Use it as a backdrop to create a character and situation based on its arrangement. Take the character on a walk through the park, surfing at the beach or painting a great masterpiece. But do not just merely hear the music. Listen, and then react to the sounds around you. NOTE: You may use ONE prop, and ONE prop ONLY. You will perform it for everyone at your next class as a graded assignment.

Application #2

Think about your monologue. Where does it occur? What are some possible sounds that your character might hear? Write them down, and stop to hear them with your imagination.

_____
_____
_____
_____
_____
_____
_____
_____

Think about the tone in your character's voice. What is the overall tone of your monologue? Is it calm, condescending, sincere, agitated, distrustful, hopeful, etc.?

_____
_____
_____

Imagine, if you will, a conversation with the character in your monologue. If you were standing beside your character, listening to them speak, how could you interrupt them? Write a few possible interjections or comments that you could make during the silent pauses of your monologue.

_____
_____
_____
_____
_____
_____

Lesson Four

Smell and Taste – Part One

The old saying, "that left a bad taste in my mouth" is sometimes used to show feelings of regret or sorrow, coming from the knowledge that one has done something wrong. It does not mean that something tasted bad in one's mouth. It just represents an emotional state of ill will. Likewise, the statement, "that stinks" could refer to either a pair of smelly gym socks or perhaps something offensive, disappointing or unjust has just taken place. Sayings like these would suggest that the senses of taste and smell are closely linked to the recollection of current emotions and even distant memories. How so?

Have you ever caught the hint of smoke in the air and suddenly, you relived the camping trip with your family when you burnt your finger roasting marshmallows over an open fire? Or has the fragrant scent of a single rose ever taken you back to that sunny, spring day when you hunted Easter eggs with your cousins in the backyard at your grandparent's house? The sense of smell can be a powerful tool for emotional recall, triggering the memories of long-forgotten events or experiences; some good and some bad. But how can you, as an actor, tap into that tool when you are standing on a stage, and there is not a hint of smoke or even the fragrance of flowers wafting in the breeze? By becoming very aware of your surroundings now, that is how. If your nose works, then start paying attention to the smells around you; whether you are at home, school, work, the mall or anywhere. And then file those scents away, because you will use them one day. The memory of how a freshly cut rose smells will help lend a realistic look to a performance, even if the actor is only holding a plastic flower. They must believe, and it will be. When that character takes a whiff of that rose, the audience should think, "Ah, springtime is in the air."

Exercise One:

You will don a blindfold. Once you find a partner, they will parade an assortment of scented

ACT ONE

objects in front of your nasal passages. You must take a whiff, guess the object and state what memory or visual image it brings to your mind. Your partner, being careful not to divulge what the objects are, will record your observations in the sections below in your own workbook. Once you are done, give the blindfold to your partner. It is now their turn.

Object #1 _____

Memory/Visual Image
_____
_____
_____

Object #2 _____
Memory/Visual Image
_____
_____
_____

Object #3 _____
Memory/Visual Image
_____
_____
_____

The sense of smell is not the only "star" in this lesson. Below the nose, and just as important, you will find the tongue and its wonderful ability to taste. If you have ever been hungry enough, and thought about your favorite food, chances are your mouth watered with excitement and anticipation. This is an example of your mind remembering the taste of the food, and responding by activating your salivary glands. Drool occurs. When the sensory recalls of taste are combined with smell, a cup of cold water can magically transform into a steaming, rich cup of coffee; especially in the hands of an experienced actor. But this brings up an interesting question. We can smell coffee. We can taste coffee. We can smell a rose. But can we taste a rose? I hope not. So, is the sensory recall of taste limited to bringing only food and beverages to life?

No, not at all! Even if a scene is set on a chilly autumn day or on a rickety fisherman's wharf, you can still use the sensory recall of taste to establish those settings as real, in your

Smell and Taste – Part One

mind. How? An actor cannot, and should not, eat rotting autumn leaves or drink water taken from the ocean, right? Right! But you can remember the food items associated with that season or geographical location.

Exercise Two:

Take time to write four foods or tastes that you associate with the following season and geographical location. Share your answers with the class.

Autumn

_____
_____
_____
_____

Ocean

_____
_____
_____
_____

By remembering the food items associated with autumn, for example, you can transport yourself directly to that season. For example, autumn makes me think of hot apple cider, candy corn, pumpkin pie and so on. Once I have those items in my mind, certain emotions are then activated by memories of past events that occurred during that time of year. Hot apple cider reminds me of the chill that hangs in the air and the rustle of leaves underfoot; candy corn takes me back to the excitement and wonder of Halloween as a small child, and pumpkin pie symbolizes time well-spent with loved ones during the holidays. Once I have set these memories firmly in place, my mind is ready to apply those feelings to the stage. Yes, in the skin of a different character, but the base emotions have been poured out like cement, and they are ready to be built memory upon memory.

Homework Assignment Four:

Over the next week, you will be asked to complete the following smell and taste sensory diary. Be unique in your choices of day/time and be thorough in your comments. Do not choose a time when you are sitting alone in your bedroom. Instead, choose the grocery store, a locker room, a restaurant, a hair salon, etc. Think outside the box. It will be a graded assignment.

ACT ONE

Day	Location	Smell/Taste	Emotions/Memories
1			
2			
3			
4			
5			
6			
7			

Lesson Five

Smell and Taste – Part Two

In our last lesson, we learned how to use the sense of taste to establish the setting for a character, either geographical or seasonal. This lesson, I would like to introduce another way of using the sense of taste to create the character itself. Let us apply taste to personality types or stereotyping.

What are the four main taste receptors?

1. _____
2. _____
3. _____
4. _____

Recently, a fifth taste receptor was identified by both the scientific and culinary worlds, although it has been around since the creation of mankind. It is called "umami." Umami is a Japanese word which means "pleasant, savory taste." It states that a food or drink item is rich, creamy and delicious. For the sake of this workshop, I would like to add one more taste receptor—bland.

So now we have six taste receptors: bitter, sour, salty, sweet, umami and bland. How can we apply the sensory recall of these six different tastes to personality types or stereotyping?

ACT ONE

Exercise One:

Complete the matching game below by drawing a line from the taste receptors to their possible mates, in your opinion.

1. Bitter   A. Little Child
2. Sour   B. Old Person
3. Salty   C. Ex-Convict
4. Sweet   D. Army General
5. Umami   E. Accountant
6. Bland   F. Runway Model

Explain your reasons for matching some of them below.

_____
_____
_____
_____
_____

Your matches may differ from someone else's matches, and that is okay. Is it not interesting how we assign certain stereotypes to certain people based on our own past experiences with them? A trained and observant actor can use those stereotypes to their advantage when building the layers of a new character. However, they must be careful not to allow that stereotype to completely define that character. It should be viewed more like a condiment, mustard or mayonnaise, giving that character some extra flavor. Not depth. The depth of a character will be determined by their socioeconomic environment and motivation, both past and present.

But it is still fun to play with these stereotypes.

Smell and Taste – Part Two

Exercise Two:

You will be given six small containers. Inside each container, you will find various food items. You must taste each item, and record your facial expressions, as you witness them, in the mirror that will be provided for you. Do you smile or frown? Do you purse your lips or suck in your cheeks? Do you furrow your brow or squint up your eyes? Do you wrinkle your nose or flare your nostrils? How does each taste make you feel? The key to this exercise is careful observation. If you have any food allergies, please let your teacher know.

Sour Candy

Alum

Salt

Honey

Sausage

White Bread

ACT ONE

Exercise Three:

Choose one of the nursery rhymes below, you will each create a character using one of the taste receptors we have discussed during this lesson: bitter, sour, salty, sweet, umami or bland. Use the facial expressions that you just recorded in Exercise Two for that specific taste experience. IMPORTANT NOTE: Do not rely on those facial expressions alone. Remember to carry your taste theme throughout the entire body by using specific body movements or gestures. Is your character bitter? Then perhaps they should stand in a defensive posture, arms folded across the chest. Is your character salty? Then perhaps placing your hands on your hips might help. Have fun! Make your character reek of that certain taste receptor. You will perform your nursery rhyme for the class.

Taste Receptor Chosen: _____

Mary had a little lamb,
Whose fleece was white as snow.
And everywhere that Mary went,
The lamb was sure to go.
He followed her to school one day,
Which was against the rules.
It made the children laugh and play,
To see a lamb at school.

Jack and Jill went up the hill,
To fetch a pail of water.
Jack fell down and broke his crown,
And Jill came tumbling after.
Up Jack got, and home did trot,
As fast as he could caper;
To old Dame Dob, who patched his nob
With vinegar and brown paper.

The itsy-bitsy spider climbed up the waterspout.
Down came the rain
and washed the spider out.
Out came the sun
and dried up all the rain
and the itsy-bitsy spider climbed up the spout again.

Smell and Taste – Part Two

Pat-a-cake, pat-a-cake, baker's man.
Bake me a cake as fast as you can;
Pat it and shape it and mark it with "B",
And bake it in the oven for baby and me.
Patty cake, patty cake, baker's man.
Bake me a cake as fast as you can;
Roll it up, roll it up;
And throw it in a pan!

There is no homework assignment for this week.

Application #3

Step into your monologue for a second. Close your eyes. Get your bearings, even with your eyes closed. Can you feel the room or setting around you? Slowly, introduce the sounds of the room into your mind. Are you there yet? If you are, then can you smell anything? What scents might be present where you are? Do you smell cheap perfume, cigarette smoke, musty leaves, fresh bread, etc.? Write them down.

_____
_____
_____
_____
_____
_____
_____

How do those scents make you feel?

_____
_____
_____
_____
_____
_____
_____

ACT ONE

Circle the taste receptor that best describes your character.

Bitter   Sour   Salty   Sweet   Umami   Bland

Explain your answer.

_____
_____
_____
_____
_____

Lesson Six

Touch

Tactile, the sense of touch, in my opinion, is the most important sensory recall weapon in any actor's arsenal. It is ten times stronger than any other sense, and it affects everything you will do. Years ago, I was coaching a young actress to play a prostitute whose presence had been requested by King Solomon in his palace. Her stage directions were simple, walk down the center aisle of a small church sanctuary straight toward the stage. Easy, right? Oh, but it is so much more than mindlessly following stage directions. The audience expects to see a young, frightened woman timidly approaching the throne of a mighty Israeli king, not an actress merely "going through the motions" to reach the end of her scene. In addition to the senses of sight and smell, I encouraged this actress to tap into her sensory recall for touch. How did we achieve that?

I asked her to use her imagination, and pay attention to key tactile words within the text of the dialogue.

Exercise One:

Read the following paragraph from the short sketch, "Split Decision" by Cheryl Cruse Weston below, and fill in the blanks below.

The guards led us down a long hallway that seemed to stretch on forever. The marble floor felt cool beneath our dusty feet, a welcome feeling after such a hot day. I felt small in there, pathetic and unworthy among the rich trappings. And yet, I must admit, a part of me wanted to belong…to leave my wretched life behind me and start all over again. But who was I kidding? No one would ever give me a second chance like that. As we approached the throne room, my heart leaped higher into my throat almost choking me with fear. King Solomon was the wisest man in all the land of Israel, and maybe even beyond, what would I say to him? How can I make him believe my story is true?

ACT ONE

Write the key sensory words that can assist you with touch.

_____ _____

_____ _____

I encouraged the actress to concentrate on her feet for this sketch. Why? From the text, we can deduce that her character is barefoot. As a prostitute in biblical times, she would have been poor and unable to afford sandals or footwear. While the actress performed the sketch barefoot on carpet, she imagined that her feet felt dry and dusty from the long, hot trek to the palace in Jerusalem. The dry, dusty feeling was magnified by the cool, smooth marble floor of the imaginary hallway that seemed to stretch on forever, reminding her that she did not belong there. She was a lowly prostitute, not worthy to stand in the presence of such a wise king. The actress conveyed that impression starting with the bottom of her feet, and then let those emotions spread to the top of her head. But it does not always have to be a physical touch that stimulates your sensory recalls. It can be a change in temperature too.

Exercise Two:

Imagine you have been stranded at the North Pole, miles from civilization, and have little in the way of protective clothing. You find a small shelter huddling among an outcropping of rocks. How can you convey to your audiences that you are cold? Write down a few ideas, and then share them with the class.

_____

_____

_____

_____

Exercise Three:

Find a partner. You have just been stranded, and left behind by your fellow explorers. You will be asked to simulate the list of environments below by drawing upon your combined sensory recalls of past temperatures and tactile exposures. They will not be called out in any certain order, so be prepared.

North Pole
Cave
Desert
Rain forest
Ocean
Thicket

Touch

Discuss your choices with your peers. What, if anything, did you learn for next time?

_____
_____
_____
_____

Exercise Four:

There will be four shoe boxes with a hole on one end. Take turns, slipping your hands through the hole, to feel the objects inside. No peeking! Each object will represent a different tactile experience. Write down several possibilities for what each object might be by using your imagination alone. You will share your observations with the class.

Object #1   Object #2
_____   _____
_____   _____
_____   _____

Object #3   Object #4
_____   _____
_____   _____
_____   _____

Exercise Five:

Tape out a 2x3 foot rectangle, giving yourself plenty of room to move around and not collide with your neighbors. The rectangle is your area. Take your shoes and socks off. Your teacher will call out a series of different tactile surfaces to walk on from slick, ice patches to hot sand. Experiment and use your imagination. Have fun!

ACT ONE

Homework Assignment Six:

It is my goal for you to become more aware of your physical surroundings. Sit in your bedroom or living room, and look around you. Without physically touching an object, use the memories of your past tactile encounters with that object to describe how it feels. Is it warm, rough, hard, cold, soft, bumpy, sharp, smooth, etc.? We live in a world full of different textures and temperatures, all ripe for the touching. You need to train yourself to recall these textures without physically touching them. It is a fun game that I like to play by myself when I am driving down the road. I see a street pole and think, "smooth." I see a fence post and think, "rough." I see grass and think, "prickly." I see a cat and think, "fuzzy." I see an oil stain on the pavement and think, "slimy."

Record your observations below.

Item_____   Item_____

Adjective_____   Adjective_____

Item_____   Item_____

Adjective_____   Adjective_____

Item_____   Item_____

Adjective_____   Adjective_____

Item_____   Item_____

Adjective_____   Adjective_____

Item_____   Item_____

Adjective_____   Adjective_____

Item_____   Item_____

Adjective_____   Adjective_____

Do not let your observations stop with this assignment. Start paying more attention to the tactile stimuli around you. If you are truly serious about acting, these sensory recalls will pay off for you one day, big time! This will be a graded assignment.

Touch

Application #4

Step into the setting of your monologue and look around. Using the tactile game from your homework assignment above, seek out the visual stimuli in your virtual world, and describe how they might feel.

Item_____   Item_____

Adjective_____   Adjective_____

Item_____   Item_____

Adjective_____   Adjective_____

Item_____   Item_____

Adjective_____   Adjective_____

Item_____   Item_____

Adjective_____   Adjective_____

Remember these adjectives, especially if your character must interact with one of these imaginary props or set pieces.

What is the temperature? Has it been raining or is it sunny outside? Is there a breeze, either natural or man made?

_____
_____
_____
_____
_____
_____

How would your character be dressed? Would their clothing be scratchy, heavy, soft or lightweight?

_____
_____
_____
_____

ACT ONE

Break Out of Your Comfort Zone

Lesson Seven

Spirit

The spirit is the invisible part of a person that contains their personality, true grit, and je ne sais quoi. Their soul. You can be proficient at sensory recall, but if your spirit is being held hostage by fear or pride, then your acting will be one dimensional. In order to achieve a sincerely brilliant performance, your spirit must be free to soar. Unfortunately, many actors never reach this point in their "careers." They remain stuck on an average acting plateau because they are unwilling to let their spirits run free. How can one climb above the average performance? I believe it is through the combined process of bursting and being.

BURSTING

Did you know that you are fearfully and wonderfully made? Whether you believe in God or not, look at yourself. You are an amazing creation. One hundred years ago, you did not even exist! And yet, here you sit. Breathing. Blood pumping. Thoughts processing. Stomach growling. Amazing! You may disagree with me, but you do have a purpose in this life. Contrary to popular opinion, you are not some blob of tissue or amoeba floating aimlessly through this world. You are an extraordinary work of art! So, live like it. Shine like a brilliant light on top of a mountain. Do not hold back! As an actor, you cannot afford to hold back. You must be adventurous and vulnerable whenever you are on the stage. Make a fool of yourself. If not, then you will fail because your spirit will be trapped within the confines of your comfort zone.

The comfort zone is a state of mind within which a person hides in an anxiety-neutral condition with no sense of risk to themselves. Once trapped in this zone, a person will become self-conscious, concerned about how they look, how they sound and even how the scene "should go." They will second guess every little move they make, and it will show through their hesitation. They will appear stiff and unnatural like a mannequin. Truthfully, we have all been guilty of living in this comfort zone, or safety bubble, at some point during our lives. But

ACT ONE

as an actor, it would be harmful for you to take up permanent residence there. Growth will only occur when you take risks and step out of your comfort zone, and shine.

Do you currently reside in a comfort zone or safety bubble?
Yes _____ No _____ Sometimes _____
Are you willing to move?
Yes _____ Yes _____ Yes _____

So, you have packed your bags and forwarded your mail to your new address outside the comfort zone. Now what? I hate to disappoint you, but saying you want to leave the comfort zone and doing it are two different balls of wax. At first, you might think that you have successfully moved, but it will take determination and willpower not to go back again. This journey might hurt a little bit, and cause you some minor discomfort or embarrassment along the way, but it will be worth the risk. Let us start working to burst that bubble that has restricted you for so many years.

What are you afraid of? Share your answers with the class.
_____
_____

Exercise One:

Everyone will sit in a circle. Follow the leader and their movements as they call out "bug in the ground," "bug in your face," 'bug in the tree," "bug in the space." And end with "all over the place." The round will become faster and faster until everyone who cannot keep up, drops out. Be prepared, you may be asked to perform this exercise solo.

Exercise Two:

Everyone will walk around the room, constantly changing the shapes of their bodies, exploring unusual poses as some music plays. The teacher at any point will stop the music, at which point all the actors freeze in their current poses. You will each be asked to justify your pose. For example, if your arm is raised, you might say, "I'm flying a kite" or "I'm painting a wall." Once everyone has justified their position, the teacher will restart the music, and the game starts all over again. Imagination is a plus!

SPIRIT

Exercise Three:

Everyone will stand in a circle, and follow the teacher's movements. If you are not familiar with this game, it will not take you long to learn the words and movements.

(Raise arms over head) Form banana. Form, form banana. Form banana. Form, form banana. (Lower arms to sides) Peel banana. Peel, peel banana. Peel banana. Peel, peel banana. (Jump up and down) Go banana. Go, go banana. Go banana. Go, go banana.

(Raise arms over head) Form potato. Form, form potato. Form potato. Form, form potato. (Lower arms to sides) Peel potato. Peel, peel potato. Peel potato. Peel, peel potato. (Stomp in circle) Mash potato. Mash, mash potato. Mash potato. Mash, mash potato.

(Raise arms over head) Form an orange. Form, form an orange. Form an orange. Form, form an orange. (Lower arms to sides) Peel an orange. Peel, peel an orange. Peel an orange. Peel, peel an orange. (Squeeze your neighbor to the right) Squeeze an orange. Squeeze, squeeze an orange. Squeeze an orange. Squeeze, squeeze an orange.

(Raise arms over head) Form the corn. Form, form the corn. Form the corn. Form, form the corn. (Lower arms to sides) Shuck the corn. Shuck, shuck some corn. Shuck the corn. Shuck, shuck the corn. (Clap hands) Pop the corn. Pop, pop the corn. Pop the corn. Pop, pop the corn.

(Get down on all fours) Form the cow. Form, form the cow. Form the cow. Form, form the cow. (Roll over on your back) Tip the cow. Tip, tip the cow. Tip the cow. Tip, tip the cow. (Shake arms and legs in air) Have a cow! Have, have a cow! Have a cow! Have, have a cow!

BEING

Just as Psalms 46:10 states, "Be still, and know that I am God," so should the actor declare, "Be still, and know that I am the character." Why would I write this? After all, it sounds disrespectful to the word of God. But it is not. Too often, I see actors who never fully dive into their characters. Hesitation and doubt ruin their performances, either due to a lot of tension (refer to Lesson One, Relaxation), a lack of bursting bubbles or possibly even both. They report not knowing what to do with their hands, their feet or their entire body. There is this irresistible urge to always be "doing" something, even though they do not know what, instead of just "being" in the situation. They need to stop all the silly, forced acting and just be. Sounds easy, right? Sadly, the state of "being' is very difficult to achieve for some actors.

According to Eric Morris, in his book *No Acting Please*, published by Ermor Enterprises, 1995, "Being is a state you work to achieve. To be, you must find out what you feel and express it totally. Let one impulse lead to another without intellectual editing, including all the life that is going on – the interruptions, interferences, and distractions." If you have trouble expressing your personal feelings, how can you expect to crawl into the skin of another character and express their feelings? You must first work on yourself.

ACT ONE

Exercise Four:

Sit comfortably on the floor. Rest your hands lightly on your thighs or knees. Close your eyes. Breathe in. Breathe out. Relax your muscles. Be still, and allow your mind to dwell on these four statements.

- I am _____.
- I want _____.
- I need _____.
- I feel _____.

Listen to your slow and steady breathing. Feel your heart beating strongly in your chest, and revel in the fact that you are gloriously alive. Fill in the blanks for these four statements repeatedly in your mind. Get in tune with yourself at this moment. Who are you? What is it that makes you tick?

Exercise Five:

As a group, you will be positioned around the room, some standing, and some sitting. It is a waiting room. The teacher will provide a few props for you to play with like magazines and brochures. You can have electronic devices if you limit their use. As your name is called, then you may leave the scene. Do not force yourself to act like you are waiting. Remember the statements above, and just be.

Homework Assignment Seven:

What are the things that keep you from leaving your comfort zone?

_____
_____
_____
_____
_____
_____
_____
_____

Do something this week that is completely outside your comfort zone. Maybe it is meeting someone new or volunteering for something you would not normally volunteer for. Maybe it is something completely off the wall like going to the store with your pants inside out and your shirt on backwards. But do something, and record it on the next page.

SPIRIT

What did you do?
_____
_____
_____
_____
_____

How did it make you feel?
_____
_____
_____
_____
_____
_____
_____
_____
_____

You will share your experience at your next class. It will be a graded assignment, so make it a good one! And for bonus points, take a picture as evidence!

Note: Do not forget to have your parent and/or guardian fill out the permission form, at the back of the book, for your observational field trip. The location of this trip will be determined by your teacher, but make it a public location where the opportunity for human observation is plentiful.

Application #5

Fill in the blanks below from your character's point of view, as though you were in their shoes right now. Quiet your mind, and just be in the moment.

I am _____.

I want _____.

I need _____.

I feel _____.

ACT ONE

What does the character in your monologue want? Is it obvious from the dialogue?

_____
_____
_____
_____

What does your character need, even if they are not aware of that need?

_____
_____
_____
_____

How do their wants and needs make them feel? Do they conflict?

_____
_____
_____
_____

By this time, you should be familiar with your script. Attempt to set it down as you rehearse. Refer to it as needed, only.

Lesson Eight

Observation

It has been said that imitation is the sincerest form of flattery, and it is true. But do not plan on imitating the acting style of your favorite actor or actress for the rest of your life. If you do, you will never make it far in the theatre. For this lesson, I want you to understand the difference between imitation and observation.

Imitation is the act of mimicking or reproducing something. Observation is the process of watching something carefully to gather information about it. As a successful actor, you must make close observation a part of your daily life. Observe everything around you from sights, sounds, tastes, smells, textures, and people. Yes, people. I often finds myself participating in my favorite pastime, people watching. During my college days, as a theatre student at Missouri State University, I worked as a loss prevention officer for a major store at the local mall. I spent hours, back then, watching people on their closed-circuit cameras, and I filed all those observations away into my mental vault. I studied how people interacted with each other, how they acted when alone and even how they moved. Did you know that you can tell a lot about a person by the way they carry themselves when they walk? Some people carry their upper torsos behind their hips; some people bounce on their toes, some people lurch more to one side, etc. Hand gestures vary too. I once observed a rather wealthy woman who was preoccupied with the rings on her fingers and her long, manicured nails. Absent-mindedly, she would play with these objects while engaged in idle conversation. I filed that information away and retrieved it when creating a rich, affluent character for my final monologue in an advanced acting class at MSU. I got an A. I did not imitate this woman, per se. I just observed her hand gestures, and used them to create a new "person." And you can do the same thing.

ACT ONE

Exercise One:

We are going on an observational field trip to a local mall. Please ask your parents to fill out the permission slip at the back of the book. Bring your Kitchen Sink workbook with you. Do not forget to bring a pen/pencil and spending money if you want to get something to eat/drink as well.

Discuss the following body positions before you begin your observations.

Foot Placement

1. _____
2. _____
3. _____

Feet Position

1. _____
2. _____
3. _____

Leg Stride

1. _____
2. _____
3. _____

Knee Position

1. _____
2. _____
3. _____

Hip Position

1. _____
2. _____
3. _____

OBSERVATION

Shoulder Position

1. _____
2. _____
3. _____

Arm Position

1. _____
2. _____
3. _____

Hand Position

1. _____
2. _____
3. _____

Head Position

1. _____
2. _____
3. _____

Move to three different vantage points as you sit watching the people pass by. Record your observations.

Location #1

_____

Observations

_____
_____
_____
_____

ACT ONE

Location #2

Observations

Location #3

Observations

OBSERVATION

There will be no homework assignment this week. Just keep working on your observations of the sights, sounds, tastes, touches, scents and people around you. See you next week!

Application #6

Think about your character. Is there someone in your life who reminds you of your character? Perhaps, they are like your mother, an uncle, your best friend, a past teacher or the creepy guy who works down at the gas station near your house. Think about it for a second. No one will judge you for your choices because they are neither right or wrong. Write down a few possible resemblances, ranking them in order of least to most.

Least Resembles
_____

Somewhat Resembles
_____

Most Resembles
_____

Now concentrate on your choices for "somewhat" and "most." Describe how they remind you of your character. Are you basing that decision on their physical appearance or on their personality?
_____
_____

Take a closer look at your "most" choice. Pick one observable characteristic that really stands out. It might be a certain gesture, habit, mannerism or style of speech. For example, your old English teacher had a habit of tugging on his chin whiskers or your next-door neighbor constantly wipes her hands on her shirt tail for no reason at all. What did you choose?
_____

Run through your monologue. Find a creative way to assimilate that characteristic into your character. It will feel very awkward at first, but keep trying. If it still feels awkward, then scratch that characteristic and try another one. If that character reminds you of more than one person, then use your observational skills to blend those two people together. Your character will become more interesting to watch. It will not be just you on the stage spitting out your memorized lines. Try it!

ACT ONE

Don't Be Afraid To Improvise

Lesson Nine

Improvisation

Improvisation has recently gained the reputation of a fast-paced, high-energy comedy club or show, such as the popular "Whose Line Is It Anyway." But it is so much more than a club or show built around comedy for the masses. I would fail in my duties as a drama teacher if I skipped over improvisation because it is a specific skill that should be studied and nurtured by all actors, from the novice to the most seasoned professional. It taps into the natural ability of all people to create characters and dialogue in the heat of the moment, playing a vital role in more advanced theatre studies. This skill is so important to keep the performance moving forward when lines are bungled beyond recognition. After all, the show must go on.

I know what you are going to say. Believe me; I hear it all the time. You are going to say, "But I cannot do improvisation!" Well, listen closely because I say, "You can, and you must!" You must burst that bubble of your comfort zone! Tap into that part of your brain that rarely gets used, and yet it is the most powerful tool you will ever have to build self-confidence in your performance as an actor. Do I expect you to be funny every time? No. Do I expect you to be witty and clever every time? Of course, not! True improvisation is more than the clichés you see at the local comedy club or on television. It combines active listening and a conscious awareness of other actors on the stage with a sense of spontaneity. In simple layman's terms, just wing it! Do not allow yourself to get bogged down in technique or fancy words, and do not worry about how silly you might feel or look while learning the art of improvisation. Simply rely on your sensory recalls and exist (or be) in the moment. And above all, have fun!

ACT ONE

Exercise One:

You will be given a series of spoken words, one at a time. Without deliberation or forethought, write down the first word of association that comes to your mind.

1._____ 2._____
3._____ 4._____
5._____ 6._____
7._____ 8._____

Find a partner. First, read to them your words of association from above, one at a time, and record their responses below in the same numerical order. Last, let them read their words of association, from above, to you, and they will record your responses in their workbooks.

1._____ 2._____
3._____ 4._____
5._____ 6._____
7._____ 8._____

Discuss how your words are similar, and how they are different. Remember, it is okay to be different.

Exercise Two:

Players begin a scene with one player acting as director. At any time, the director will ask a player to say a line differently by tooting a horn or ringing a bell. The performer must say a completely different line and then justify it in the scene. The scene will run to its logical conclusion or end when someone calls "end scene."

Exercise Three:

Two players tell a story, taking turns. One storyteller has only good, positive things to say like, "Once upon a time there lived a beautiful Queen in the Kingdom of Bologna." Then the other storyteller, who only has negative remarks, chimes in, "Who had five ugly daughters." The first storyteller, "Fortunately, the Queen decreed that all the men in the kingdom have their eyes gouged out on the 20th of May." The other player adds, "Ironically Pastrami, the kingdom next door, declared war on the 21st of May." The first player, "Thankfully, it was a short war, because the Pastramians were deaf and could not hear the tornado sirens blaring."

IMPROVISATION

Exercise Four:

Two people start a scene. At any time, someone will yell, "freeze." When "freeze" is called, all players freeze. The person who called it comes up, tags one of the people out of the scene and takes their exact physical position. When they unfreeze, that new player begins a completely different unrelated scene based on that exact physical position. This new scene continues until someone else calls "freeze," and so it continues.

Homework Assignment Eight:

Your teacher will give you a picture containing a geographical location and/or situation. Analyze the photo. Are there people in the photo? If so, who are they? What feelings are evoked by their appearance? What sensory recalls are stimulated? Imagine how these people ended up in that location or situation. Fill out the character worksheet below, creating a character of your own. At the beginning of the next class, you will be allowed to rearrange the classroom to look like the photo in the envelope. You may bring any props or costumes necessary to help you recreate that corner of the world. Your teacher will then move among you, posing as a freelance photojournalist, interviewing everyone he or she meets. You will be expected to answer the questions as the character that you have created. Not as yourself. Nothing will be rehearsed or "staged." It will be sincere improvisation at its finest. And it will be a graded assignment.

1. What is your character's name?

   _____

2. How old is your character?

   _____

3. Where is your character from?

   _____

4. What circumstance brought your character to their situation today? Be detailed in your answer.

   _____
   _____
   _____
   _____
   _____

ACT ONE

5. Does your character have a goal in life? If so, what is it? It can be something colossal like winning the Nobel Peace Prize or something minute like owning a flea circus.

6. Is your character afraid of something? If so, what is it?

7. What is your character's most prized earthly possession that they carry with them?

8. Describe something miscellaneous about your character.

Lesson Ten

Blocking and Movement

Blocking is the choreographed movement of an actor, or actors, during a play or film. The term, "blocking" came from the 19th-century director, Sir W.S. Gilbert, who once worked out the movement of his plays on a miniature stage using wooden blocks to represent each of the actors. Today, blocking tells actors where they should move for the proper dramatic effect and ensures adequate sightlines for the audience. But blocking is much more than just an actor's movement around a stage. If handled correctly, it should reveal something to the audience about the character's personalities, and ultimately creates a "snapshot" that successfully moves the plotline forward. Study the images below. Take note how each one is showing a moment frozen in time.

ACT ONE
RULES OF MOVEMENT

1. **Movement must be motivated.**

   Why is your character moving? How does the movement further the performance?

2. **Movement must be simplified.**

   Is the movement complimentary to the performance? Does it distract from the storyline?

3. **Movement must be heightened.**

   Does your action reach everyone in the audience? Are you using your space to its full capacity?

4. **Movement must define your character.**

   Does it define your age, size and personality? How is your non-verbal stage business?

5. **Movement must stay open to the audience.**

   Are you masking movements that the audience must see, even those people on the back row?

6. **Movement must adjust to other characters on the stage.**

   What is your body language in relation to other characters onstage? Is there give and take between actors? Is there any stage business or action in between movements?

Before we dive any deeper into the world of movement, we must travel back through time to the origin of theatre in Greece circa 700 BC, where the first theatrical building was called a theatron or the "seeing place." It was a large, open-air structure constructed on the slope of a hill, perfect for acting, choral performances, and religious rites. The original stages were raked, meaning that their lowest points were next to the audience. When an actor moved away from the audience, he or she moved uphill or "upstage." And when they moved toward the audience, they were moving downhill or "downstage." Over the years, the physical structure of the stage has changed with the introduction of the proscenium, thrust, arena, round and black-box style theatres. But the nine acting areas have pretty much stayed the same.

Exercise One:

The first thing an actor must learn about blocking is the main acting areas of a stage. Label the diagram on the next page. Ask your teacher for help, if you need it.

Blocking and Movement

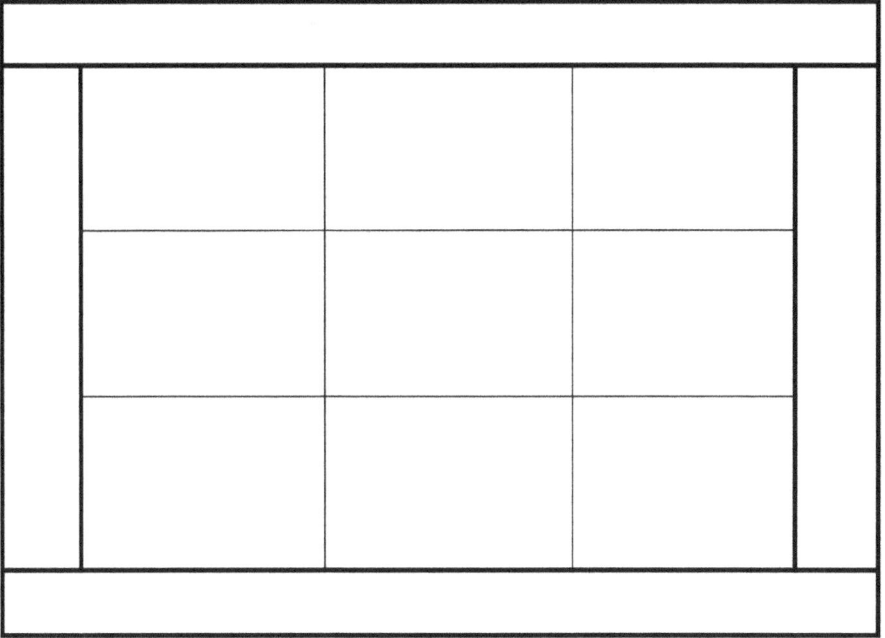

FIVE MAIN BODY POSITIONS

1.   **Full Front:** This position creates an atmosphere of intimacy. The character is facing the audience, inviting their complicity or involvement.

2.   **Quarter Turn:** This position offers a high degree of intimacy but with less emotional involvement than the full-front position.

3.   **Profile:** This position is more remote than the quarter turn, the character in profile seems unaware of being observed, lost in their thoughts. It is also beneficial in confrontational scenes between two characters.

4.   **Three-Quarter Turn:** This position is useful for conveying a character's unfriendly or antisocial feelings, for, in effect, the character is partially turning their back on the audience, rejecting their interest.

5.   **Full Back:** This is the most anonymous of all positions, often used to suggest a character's alienation from the world. When a character has their back to the audience, we can only guess what is taking place internally, conveying a sense of concealment, or mystery.

ACT ONE

Exercise Two:

Label the acting positions, assuming the audience is at the bottom of the page

_____   _____   _____   _____   _____

BASIC MOVEMENTS

1. Cross

A cross occurs when an actor moves from one place to another on the stage. A direct cross shows determination and strength while a curved cross shows thoughtfulness, ease or uncertainty.

2. Counter-cross

Countering is the act of adjusting your position on stage to conform to another actor's cross. If an actor is standing in conversation with you and then crosses in front of you to the other side of the room, you would shift your weight from the upstage foot and with one or two small steps turn so that you are facing them again. It should be done very easy and inconspicuously.

3. Dressing the Stage

This blocking spreads the actors on the available stage space, creating a more substantial and balanced picture.

4. Turning

All turns on the stage should be executed towards the audience. If you are standing profile in the middle of the stage, facing the right, and you wish to turn and cross to the left, turn towards the audience so that your face is visible the whole time. There will be, however, times when your back must face the audience at the discretion of the director.

5. Entrances and Exits

Entrances and exits are very important to the effectiveness of an actor. The actor should

Blocking and Movement

always make an emphatic entrance (unless directed to be sneaky) from at least six feet in the wings and exit in character at least six feet offstage. In this way, you will be in character as you come into view on the stage, and you will be walking in the right rhythm.

6. **Levels**
Levels can give the audience added visual excitement and create balance in unusual ways. They can include trap doors, the floor, low stools, chairs, cubes, high stools, ladders, risers, platforms and second floors. Levels can also be used to denote which character is more dominate at any given moment in a scene.

7. **Arms and Legs**
Be sure to use your upstage foot whenever you start a cross across the stage. And whenever you pick up an object, use your upstage hand.

8. **Stage Business**
Stage business is the smaller activities that actors do while saying their lines that help build character. These activities usually require additional props such as cigarettes, cell phone, nail polish, drinks, and so on. Stage business must remain true to that character and never distract the audience's attention away from the main action of the play.

Exercise Three:

An actor moves into position, either on a chair, the floor, in a doorway or among a crowd of people. They freeze in an interesting position like they were caught in the middle of doing something. One by one, the other actors move into that same space and freeze doing something similar but very different than the first actor. Eventually, a picture develops. It might be a party scene, a session of Congress, an assembly line or a crime scene. It is all up to your imagination. Remember the importance of body position.

Exercise Four:

You will all be placed within one of the nine acting areas of a stage. There will be obstacles in your path, such as other humans, props, and set pieces. You must follow your stage directions, as they are called out to you. If you make a mistake, then you will be asked to repeat that move until you get it correct. The goal of this exercise is to act out an entire scene without dialogue, just by blocking and movement alone.

ACT ONE

Homework Assignment Nine:

Study the photos and answer the following questions. This will be a graded assignment.

1. How many actors are on the stage? _____
2. How many acting levels can you see? _____
3. Name some of the body positions.

   _____
   _____

4. Where and/or who is the focus of this scene, and why?

   _____
   _____
   _____
   _____
   _____
   _____
   _____
   _____
   _____

BLOCKING AND MOVEMENT

1. How many actors are on the stage? _____
2. How many acting levels can you see? _____
3. Name some of the body positions.
   _____
   _____

4. Where and/or who is the focus of this scene, and why?
   _____
   _____
   _____
   _____
   _____
   _____

Search the Internet to find either
a movie or theatrical production
still (photo) that really grabs your
attention. Tape it here.

ACT ONE

1. How many actors are on the stage? _____
2. How many acting levels can you see? _____
3. Name some of the body positions.

   _____
   _____

4. Where and/or who is the focus of this scene, and why?

   _____
   _____
   _____
   _____

Application #7

Have you created any blocking for your monologue yet?
Yes_____   No_____   Maybe_____
What, if any, body positions do you plan to use?

_____
_____
_____
_____

How many acting levels will you use?
_____

Are you speaking to the audience, to yourself or to another character in the room?
_____

Have you thought of any "stage business"? Name some small activities that your character might perform, like picking at a small thread on their shirt, biting their nails or rubbing their own neck.

_____
_____
_____
_____

Make sure your crosses are made with purpose. Avoid drifting across the stage like a confused iceberg. Even if you have blocked your character to pace, make your pacing look crisp and purpose-driven.

Lesson Eleven

Voice – Part One

Henry Wadsworth Longfellow once said, "The human voice is the organ of the soul." The proper use of one's voice is important to the success of both the beginning actor and the well-seasoned actress. Without it, most stories could never be told, and theatres all over the world would become eerily quiet. Vocal lessons in the theatre are usually divided into two areas of study: voice and speech. Voice training focuses primarily on the vocal tone and range of the actor's voice while speech training concentrates on the actor's understanding of articulation and dialect. But, here at the Kitchen Sink, I would like to propose a simpler approach to voice training based on the following two questions:

1. Can the actor be heard and understood?
2. Is the actor painting a colorful character using their voice alone?

The answer to the first question, "Can the actor be heard and understood?" should be obvious. Of course, the audience needs to hear and understand the actor when they speak. There are two common mistakes that the beginning actor makes while onstage. First, they are often soft-spoken, relying too heavily on the acoustics of the room or the assistance of microphones. Second, they do not fully open their mouth and use proper diction, making themselves sound garbled like their cheeks are full of mush or gravel. They cannot be heard or understood, resulting in terrible consequences for both the entire show and the actor, as a performer. So how can the actor be sure that the audience can both hear and understand their performance? They must master the arts of volume and enunciation.

ACT ONE
VOLUME

It is easy for directors to shout from the back of the auditorium, "Project! You must project!" But it is harder for a novice actor to fully understand what the word, "project" means. Projection is much more than speaking loudly or yelling at the top of your lungs until you are blue in the face. Unfortunately, that is what most actor's do, and it will only lead to fatigued and strained vocal chords. True projection is a combination of relaxation exercises, proper breathing, correct posture and an awareness of the resonance in your voice.

Relaxation

We discussed relaxation at the very beginning of this workshop, but let us review it again. Think about your face, jaw, and throat for a moment. How relaxed are they whenever you are acting? You say that they are usually tense? Perhaps you are dropping your chin too much or clenching your jaws. It is important for good vocal control to maintain an open and relaxed airway, which includes the face, jaw, and throat.

Exercise One:

Practice the motions of chewing in an exaggerated manner and then gradually add humming, random sounds and words like "water bottle" or "baby buggy." Slowly reduce the degree of exaggeration of the mouth movements. This exercise will help to release excess tension in the vocal tract and laryngeal area. If done correctly, it will encourage mouth opening and reduction of tension in the jaw.

Exercise Two:

Massage your jaw at its hinge point. As you begin freeing the jaw, you may start to yawn. That is great. Keep yawning! Get a great stretch for both the jaw and the lips. Allow your newly relaxed jaw to release down for a moment and feel that space that opens under your ear as the hinge releases down. Now take your chin between your thumb and index finger. Try to move your lower jaw up and down freely. It is not as easy as it sounds.

Breathing

In daily life, most of us are used to breathing from the upper part of the chest, but that can lead to a lot of unwanted tension in the ribcage and shoulders. So, the actor must train themselves to root their breathing from the lower abdomen and back, also known as the "core." I will explain the importance of your core when we reach the topic of posture.

Voice – Part One

Exercise Three:

This exercise uses the body's natural reflex system to ensure that your breathing remains powerful without creating any unnecessary pressure. Do not hold your breath when the lungs are full. This will cause tension and pressure in the throat, preventing it from remaining open and relaxed.

1. Lie on your back with your bare feet flat on the floor and knees slightly apart, bent and pointing at the ceiling. Keep your shoulders and upper chest relaxed, with the waist and stomach muscles pulled inward toward the spine.
2. Place both hands at the bottom of your ribcage so you can feel the expansion and contraction of your lower abdomen and back as you breathe in and out.
3. Breathe in slowly through your nose and then sigh noiselessly as you exhale, expelling the air. All the movement should happen from the lower ribs only.
4. Repeat ten times, gradually deepening the breath each time.

Exercise Four:

Now we will turn our attention to the diaphragm, which is the sheet of internal skeletal muscle that extends across the bottom of your thoracic cavity. It is essentially the bedrock of your voice.

1. Remain lying on the floor and place your hands, palms down, on your abdomen.
2. Breathe in through the nose, and exhale through the mouth.
3. As you exhale, give several little pants ("huh" sounds) until you are confident that the sound is springing from the diaphragm, rather than being pushed out of the upper chest or throat.
4. You can even speak some lines of text, and notice how effortlessly you can speak when your breath is rooted, and your throat free from tension.

Posture

Correct posture and alignment of an actor's core muscles are other key elements for strong vocal production. At the turn of the century, a young actor, Frederick Alexander, created a new technique for posture that gave birth to the now widely-used neutral stance. The "Alexander Technique" forms a firm foundation for the actor's voice and also creates a blank canvas on which to develop their character's movements.

ACT ONE

Exercise Five:
1. Stand with your legs straight, but relaxed at the knees. Your feet should be facing forward, shoulder-width apart.
2. Slowly visualize your neck lengthening as the muscles in your shoulders and back release, becoming more open and relaxed.
3. Your arms should hang, relaxed, at your sides.
4. Imagine that your body is being gently pulled up by an "invisible thread" attached to the top of your head. It should make you feel even more aligned, especially in the neck and shoulders.
5. Stand in this neutral stance for 1-5 minutes.

Resonance

Resonance, what is that? It is the reinforcement of a sound by its reflection or vibration off a neighboring surface. It operates much like an echo. There are many resonators or vibrators in the human body like the chest, mouth, nose, pharynx, nasal cavities, sinuses and facial bones. The quality of one's voice depends on which area of the body contributes most to the overall resonance (we will discuss this more in Lesson Twelve, Voice Part Two). As an actor, you will need to learn how to combine different resonators, and especially to develop your chest resonance so that your vocal tone is rich. The neutral stance, above, will help you tap into that rich, chest resonance.

Exercise Six:
1. Achieve the neutral stance.
2. Relax your face. There must be no tension in the face, tongue or throat.
3. Gently hum, feeling the sound vibrate at the front of your nasal cavity and the front of your top palate.
4. Smile the sound into your cheeks.
5. Raise your eyebrows so that sound travels into your forehead.
6. Relax your face, continuing to hum.
7. Repeat.

Exercise Seven:
1. Achieve the neutral stance.
2. Place your hand just below your chest sternum or solar plexus. Gently hum, allowing the sound to vibrate in this area.
3. Place your hand on your upper chest. Allow the vibration of the hum to fill this area.
4. Repeat.

Voice – Part One

ENUNCIATION

When considering our original question of "Can the audience hear the actor?" we must also keep in mind that it is more than just an issue of volume. The audience must be able to understand what they have just heard, as well. There must be clarity to their speech. An actor may have a strong and bellowing voice, but if they rush or stumble through their lines, then their loud delivery will have been made in vain. They must enunciate and learn to pace themselves.

According to the Merriam-Webster dictionary, enunciation is the act of pronouncing words or parts of words clearly. We must visit the ABC's of vowels and consonants to learn the concept of enunciation.

Vowels

The English vowels are "a, e, i, o, u," and all possible combinations of these letters when spoken aloud. These basic vowel sounds are made by changing the positioning of the tongue and the lips around one basic shape, "ah," which can be expressed in a number of different ways. In fact, vowel sounds can often convey the emotion within the writer's words since they are longer, more open sounds that are directly connected to the breath. And the breath, in turn, is connected to the emotions.

Exercise Eight:

1. Take the neutral stance position.
2. Keep your shoulders and neck relaxed.
3. Take a deep breath into the lower abdomen, using the diaphragm.
4. Connect the out breath to a hum.
5. Without breaking the hum, push your lips forward in the "ae" shape, making the "ae" sound. Use your muscle memory to focus on the shape and feeling of your lips, tongue and mouth for this sound.
6. Relax.
7. Repeat with the "ah," "ee," "eh," "oo," "or" and "yuh" sounds.

Consonants

The consonants are the other 21 letters of the alphabet. While vowels can convey emotion, consonants can add sharpness and clarity to the spoken dialogue. They are formed by initially blocking the sound and then releasing suddenly on the explosive consonants "p" and "b," gradually on "n" and "l," and more gradually still with "s" and "z." Precision is important because a small misplacement of the tongue or lips can make a big difference to the sound.

ACT ONE

Exercise Nine:

Take the neutral stance, and work on the tongue twister below. Keep the shoulders, neck, jaw, lips, and tongue relaxed and free from any unnecessary tension. Pay close attention to the consonants and vowels.

- Betty Botter bought some butter, but she said the butter's bitter. If I put it in my batter, it will make my batter bitter. But a bit of better butter's bound to make my batter better. So, she bought a bit of butter better than her bitter butter, and she put it in her batter, and it made her batter better. So, a bit of better butter's better for a bitter batter.

Be careful not to rely on enunciation alone when delivering your lines. There is a tendency for new actors to rush through their dialogue like a speeding freight train, either because they were nervous, unprepared or there was a lack of proper relaxation beforehand. Relax. Slow down. Pace yourself. Use pauses to your advantage. Know your lines. But more importantly, immerse yourself in your character. If you can do all that, then your timing will naturally and automatically fall into place.

Homework Assignment Ten:

Choose one of the familiar tongue twisters below. Memorize it and come prepared next time to combine it with one of the following emotions: fear, anger, sorrow or joy. Make good use of your pauses and timing. You will perform it for the class as a graded assignment.

- How much wood would a woodchuck chuck if a woodchuck could chuck wood? A woodchuck would chuck all the wood he could chuck if a woodchuck would chuck wood.

- Peter Piper picked a peck of pickled peppers. A peck of pickled peppers Peter Piper picked. If Peter Piper picked a peck of pickled peppers, how many pickled peppers did Peter Piper pick?

- A tutor who tooted the flute tried to tutor two tooters to toot. Said the two to the tutor, "Is it tougher to toot or to tutor two tooters to toot?"

- I need not your needles; they're needless to me; for kneading of noodles, 'twere needless, you see. But did my neat knickers but need to be kneed, I then should have need of your needles indeed.

Voice – Part One

Application #8

Lie on your back with your feet flat on the floor and knees slightly apart, bent and pointing at the ceiling. Keep your shoulders and upper chest relaxed, with the waist and stomach muscles pulled inward toward the spine. Place both hands at the bottom of your ribcage so you can feel the expansion and contraction of your lower abdomen and back as you breathe in and out. Are you comfortable? Good. Now run your lines, from beginning to end. Notice how much richer, louder and stronger your voice sounds when lying down.

Now, stand up and assume the neutral stance. Stand with your legs straight, but relaxed at the knees. Your feet should be facing forward, shoulder-width apart. Slowly visualize your neck lengthening as the muscles in your throat and jaw become more open and relaxed. Your arms should hang, relaxed, at your sides. Imagine that your body is being gently pulled up by an "invisible thread" attached to the top of your head. It should make you feel even more aligned, especially in the neck and shoulders. Stand in this neutral stance for 1-5 minutes. Run your lines from this position. Try very hard to keep your feet "nailed" to the floor. You will be tempted to drift, but stand firm.

Were you able to achieve the same vocal quality using the neutral stance as opposed to lying down?

Yes _____   No _____
If not, why?
_____
_____
_____

Try it again. But this time, pay close attention to where your voice dwells in your body. Do you feel it vibrating in your nasal passages, your throat or your chest? Where are you placing the power of your voice? Where do you want to place it? Try changing the placement of your voice, and notice how your voice will change.

Feeling brave?

Run through your monologue again, but this time, add your blocking. It is harder to pay attention to relaxation, proper breathing, good posture and resonance when you are moving. Do not let it consume you to the point that it distracts you from the character or story you are sharing. But do be aware of it. The audience needs to hear you.

ACT ONE

Find Your Character's Voice

Lesson Twelve

Voice – Part Two

Can an actor be heard and understood? If the answer is yes, then the next question becomes "Can the actor paint a colorful character using their voice alone?" This will depend somewhat on the dialogue that the playwright has written, and on how the director instructs the actor to deliver that dialogue. But a lot of the responsibility still falls on the actor's shoulders themselves. Can they make the words on the pages of their script come alive? How willing are they to slip into their character's vocal "skin"? Could their characters have a speech impediment or speak with a twang? Perhaps they habitually spit when they stumble across a "th" or "st" sound. Are they from Little Rock, Arkansas or Dallas, Texas or Frankfurt, Germany? These are important questions that often get overlooked. Actors must become good at weaving a colorful tapestry for their character's voice, and it all begins with the thread of tone.

In Lesson Three, Hearing, we learned that tone is not what a person says, but how they say it. Simply put, it is their specific vocal quality. Every human being has a voice, but tone is what makes each voice sound unique. Tone is basically composed of the following characteristics: inflection, placement, garnish, and accent.

INFLECTION

Inflection occurs when there is change in the rhythm, emphasis, pitch or volume of an actor's voice. This characteristic is important for creating an interesting vocal canvas for characters in a play or movie. When looking at the words in a script, you, the actor should consider it an opportunity to create an exciting rollercoaster with twists and turns, rather than a boring highway that is flat and deserted. You should also avoid the pitfalls of reciting your lines from rote like a monotone robot (unless of course, you are playing a monotone robot). This will require you to be on the lookout for key words in your dialogue to emphasize, knowing that

ACT ONE

well-placed stress on certain words can change the entire meaning of a sentence (Lesson Three, Hearing). But above all, you must remain connected to your character's inner life. For example, do not be hasty and force a stereotypically timid voice on a shy character. Instead, be open to explore other vocal options for that character, instead of what might be easy and expected. Stay true to your character's back story, environmental setting, and motivation throughout the process, and you will succeed.

Exercise One:

Look at the sentence.

"I didn't tell Brenda to shut the blue door."

Notice how the meaning of that sentence can change by simply stressing or emphasizing a different word each time. Give it a try. As the stressed, underlined word changes, write your interpretation of the newly created sentence below it.

I didn't tell Brenda to shut the blue door.
_____
_____

I <u>didn't</u> tell Brenda to shut the blue door.
_____
_____

I didn't <u>tell</u> Brenda to shut the blue door.
_____
_____

I didn't tell <u>Brenda</u> to shut the blue door.
_____
_____

Voice – Part Two

I didn't tell Brenda to <u>shut</u> the blue door.

_____

_____

I didn't tell Brenda to shut the <u>blue</u> door.

_____

_____

I didn't tell Brenda to shut the blue <u>door</u>.

_____

_____

Exercise Two:

Read the sentences below using the emotions of anger, fear, doubt, determination, sarcasm, disgust, joy, pity, curiosity, indifference and regret.

"I won't do it."   "I'd love to."   "She's my friend."

Notice how each emotion can change the meaning and tone of every sentence, even though the sentences themselves did not change. That is the power of inflection at work.

PLACEMENT

Consider, if you will, the recent example of the twisting and turning roller coaster. If vocal inflection represents the track, then the placement of the voice should be considered the car that rides on top of the track. So, then what is placement? Placement is basically where your character's voice dwells or resonates within your body, which we discussed somewhat in the last lesson. It can, and should, change with each character you play. For example, for comic effect the voice could be placed in the nose, thus creating a nasally sounding villain. Perhaps it could be placed in the top of the head for a high-pitched, falsetto voice of a lady who is stereotypically a "dumb blond." For a more dramatic presentation, the voice should be placed in its natural center, the chest and/or diaphragm. There are many locations for an actor to place their voice, but here is a short list for your perusal.

ACT ONE

- Chest and/or diaphragm
- Forehead and/or top of head
- Nasal cavity and/or adenoids
- Front palate and/or behind the front teeth
- Soft palate and/or back of throat
- Lower jaw and/or under mouth floor

Each location will produce a completely different voice, so do not be afraid to experiment. But no matter where you choose to "place" your voice, remember to approach your character from a physical point of view. For example, when playing a much older person, you will need to take into consideration the physical aspects of aging. Ask yourself, "How does aging affect the person's posture and even their breathing?" and "How do those changes then affect the placement of the voice?" If you can approach your character from this point of view, your results will be more realistic.

Exercise Three:
Recite the entire alphabet, from A to Z, using each of the following suggestions.

1. Your teeth clenched together.
2. Your teeth slightly apart.
3. Your bottom jaw pulled back.
4. Your chin raised as high as possible.
5. Your chin moved as forward as possible.

Notice that the sounds produced by your voice are different with each suggestion. Why is that?

_____
_____
_____

Exercise Four:
Experiment moving your voice to different locations throughout your upper torso and head by repeating the following statement.

"Moving day has come at last. By train or plane, to Budapest."

Record your observations. Using stereotypes, what kind of character could you create with that voice?

Voice – Part Two

Chest and/or diaphragm

___

Forehead and/or top of head

___

Nasal cavity and/or adenoids

___

Front palate and/or behind the front teeth

___

Soft palate and/or back of throat

___

Lower jaw and/or under the mouth floor

___

GARNISH

Here, at the Kitchen Sink, one of the final ingredients of tone is aptly called garnish. Like a sprinkle of parsley or a sprig of mint, it can "dress" up an actor's voice and give an extra dimension to their character. It could be the addition of a simple lisp, a little gravel, a hint of rasp and even a slight stutter. These variations can be achieved by changing the placement of the tongue against the teeth, altering the shape or elasticity of the lips and strategically controlling the respirations. Once again, do not be afraid to experiment.

Exercise Five:

Revisit Exercise Four, but this time, add some "seasoning" to those placements.
Rasp
Stutter
Lisp
Stuffed nose
Broken teeth
Gravel

ACT ONE

IMPORTANT: Keep in mind that too much garnish can ruin an entire dish and an entire voice. If you add too much stutter or lisp to your voice, the audience might not be able to understand you, thus creating a gigantic problem. So, garnish to taste, and use it sparingly.

ACCENT

Every well-rounded actor should maintain a wide range of accents in their vocal library, especially for playing characters from a specific geographical area or ethnicity. But do not be fooled. Accents are not the same thing as dialects. An accent is the way different people sound, meaning the way they pronounce their words and the rhythm of their speech. A dialect describes both a person's accent and the grammatical features of the way they talk. To successfully learn an accent requires assimilating the rhythm and exact pronunciation of the vowels and consonants as they relate to that specific character. It will also require a restructuring of the muscles in your lower jaw, lips, and tongue. It may feel awkward at first and sound even worse, but do not give up. Remember, practice does make perfect.

Over the next few pages, you will learn about three accents: Mexican-Spanish accent, French accent, and East Coast Irish accent. Choose one, and practice speaking in that accent.

Mexican Spanish

Consonant clusters are sounds formed by the union of two consonants like "sw" or "tr." There are certain clusters that the average Mexican will not recognize pronouncing because the combination of those letters does not exist in the Spanish language. Here are a few rules to remember when learning to speak with a "Mexican Spanish" accent.

LL For a Spanish speaker, the consonant cluster of LL represents an indigenous sound similar to the sound produced by the letter Y in the English language. Consequently, a Mexican will inevitably pronounce "yellow" as "jeyo" and "llama" as "yama."

NG/ND In the Spanish language, words usually do not end with the English consonant cluster of NG or ND. So when a Mexican encounters a word that ends with NG or ND, they automatically drop the G, or the D, and make it end with just an N. "Lifting" will become "leefteen" and "friend" will become "fren."

RR Whenever two R's are placed next to each other in a word, like "arrow" and "barren," a Mexican will naturally trill the consonant cluster sound of RR. They will also trill a single R if the letter is placed at the beginning of such words like "rich" and "recall."

SH Remember that the "sh" sound is troublesome to many Mexicans. They simply do not have that consonant cluster in their language, and therefore substitute it with its closest phonetic relative, the sound of "ch." Hence "shower" will become "chower," "share" will become "chare" and "shallow" will become "chayo."

Voice – Part Two

ST

You will find that most Mexicans add the sound "est" at the beginning of English words that start with the consonant cluster of ST. Therefore, words like "station" will become "estation" and "stupid" will become "estupid."

TH

There are two "th" sounds in the English language: the soft "th" in "there" or "though" and the hard "th" in "with" or "think." Mexicans tend to substitute the soft "th" with a "d" sound, as in "I do not want to do dat dough." Conversely, they will substitute the hard "th" with a "t" sound, as in "I teenk dis is a torough test."

B

Keep in mind that in the Spanish language, the letters B and V are interchangeable because they sound almost exactly the same. For this reason, many Mexicans might mispronounce "video" as "bideo" and "volleyball" as "bolleyball."

G/J

The English letters G and J are pronounced very differently in the Spanish language. They do not possess the familiar "dge" or "guh" sounds, but they sound more like the "huh" sounds of an H. Those unique pronunciations are carried over into the English language when Mexicans utter words such as "George" as "Horhay" and "banjo" as "banhoe."

H

Keep in mind that the letter H is fairly silent in the Spanish language, formed at the back of the throat like they are coughing up a small hairball. So it stands to reason that the average Mexican will honor that pronunciation in English as well, making "hospital" sound like "ospital" and "somehow" sound like "someow."

I

The English letter, I, will become a long vowel when spoken by someone of Spanish descent. It is naturally pronounced as "ee," making such words as "fill" sound like "feel" and "rich" sound like "reach."

U

Another English letter, the U, will also fall victim to the long vowel sound that is common to the Spanish language. Instead of "oo," "uh" and "yew," a Mexican will only pronounce an English U as "oo," making "rut" sound like "root" and "umbrella" sound like "oombreya."

Y

In most Mexican accents, the Spanish letter Y has almost the same sound as the letter J in English. So words that begin with a Y in English such as "you," "yes" and "yesterday" will sound like "joo," "jes" and "jesterday."

Read the second sentence below. Then rewrite the sentence to how it phonetically should sound with a Mexican accent. Here is an example.

John thinks Violet should live in the red house with her yellow umbrella.

Hoe-on tinks Biolet chood lib een de rred ows wit er jello oombreya.

ACT ONE

Yes, Sharon and Randy are driving in their Jeep to Amarillo for their vacation in August.

_____

_____

French

The French language contains no diphthongs, so its vowels will always be shorter than their English counterparts. For example, the long A in "gate" will become the short E in "get." Short words that native English speakers tend to skim over or swallow will always be carefully pronounced by French speakers. The latter will say "peanoot boo-tair and zhell ee," whereas native English speakers opt for pean't butt'r 'n' jelly. Likewise, French speakers will usually not make contractions, instead of pronouncing every word: "I would go" instead of "I'd go" and "She eez reh-dee" rather than "She's ready." Here are some other vocal rules when learning a French accent.

ED A French citizen will often emphasize or stress the letters ED at the end of a verb or adjective, even if that means adding an extra syllable, such as "amazed" will become "ah may zed" or "lacked" will become "lack ed."

ER Any time an English word ends with the consonant cluster of ER, the French will undoubtedly pronounce it with an "aire" at the end. Words like "water" and "shorter" will then become "wah taire" and "shor taire."

TH Just like the Mexican character before, a person of French descent will have difficulty with the consonant cluster of TH. This combination just does not exist in the French language, so they will pronounce it with a "zee" sound, turning "that" into "zat" and "thermometer" into "zer mom eh taire."

H Typically, the H sound is always silent in French, so the common French character will pronounce the words "happy" as "appy" and "hamburger" as "am bur gaire." Once in a while, they might make a particular effort, usually resulting in an overly forceful H sound, even with words like "hour" and "honest," in which the H is oddly silent in English.

I Whenever a French person encounters a short, I sound, such as in the word "sip" they will always pronounce it with an "ee" sound, turning it into "seep." When confronted with a long I sound, like in the word "kite," they will tend to elongate it and almost turn it into a two syllable word like "ka it."

J The letter J is likely to be pronounced as "zh" like the G sound at the end of the word "massage." Consequently, English words like "juice" and "juniper" will be spoken as "zhoose" and "zhoon ee paire."

Voice – Part Two

O The short O sound actually deviates from the norm for French people because they often pronounce it two different ways. For example, the English word "cot." The French are guilty of pronouncing this word as either "cut" or "coat." It is essentially the same word and same short vowel sound, but two very polar pronunciations.

R If you will recall the consonant cluster of RR for the Mexican character above, it requires a trilling of the tongue. So does the single R for a French character. But the placement of the tongue is very different. Instead of trilling the tip of the tongue at the front of the mouth, you will need to very slightly trill the larger part of your tongue at the back of your hard palate. It will almost feel like you are attempting to swallow the R sound if performed correctly. This process is difficult to describe in written form, and sometimes can only be taught in person or by audible means.

U Oddly enough, the U sound in French is the same exact sound that we discovered in the Mexican character. Words like "full" and "tumbler" will be pronounced "fool" and "toom blaire."

Read the second sentence below. Then rewrite the sentence to how it phonetically should sound with a French accent. Here is an example.

Juliet and her brother are hungry for a thick, juicy hamburger with mustard.

Zhoolee-et and er brozer are oongree for a zik, zhoocee amboorgaire wiz moostard.

The runner was amazed that he was able to outrun the mother bear.

_____

_____

East Coast Irish

The most difficult part of learning an Irish accent, whether it is East Coast, Southwestern or Northern, is becoming familiar with the rhythm and tone of the accent. It has been described as almost lyrical in nature, more musical than American English. And their alphabet is also a lot shorter with only 12 consonants compared to our 21. Keep these facts in mind as you read the following rules for learning an East Coast Irish accent.

NG The English language is full of words that end in the consonant cluster of NG. But just like the Mexican character, that sound is dropped making words like "morning" and "walking" become "mornin" and "walkin."

ACT ONE

Sometimes, the consonant cluster of TH is pronounced as a plosive sound, which is made when part of the mouth is blocked so that no air can pass through, and the pressure increases behind the place where it is blocked, and when the air can pass through again, an abrupt sound is created. Thus changing "three" to "tree" and "thin" to "tin."

The ECI accent tends to over-pronounce the H sound in the consonant cluster of WH, making words like "whine" sound like "hwine" and "whopper" sound like "hwopper."

The short vowel sound of the letter A, in words like "map" and "glass," needs to be softened to almost an "ah" sound, like in the word "father."

When used at the beginning of an English word, a citizen from the ECI will pronounce the letter D more like the "dg" sound in the word, judge. For example, "due" will be pronounced more like "jew" and "dent" more like "gent."

The sound for the letter I in ECI is very like the American English sound "oi." Such words like "night," "like" and "Ireland" are pronounced as "noit," "loik" and "Oireland."

Always make sure to strongly articulate the L sound when recreating an ECI accent.

Another important phonetic rule is the letter R. A character with an ECI accent tends to place their R sounds more forward and higher in their mouths. They are very conscious of pronouncing every R, whether it sits at the beginning, middle or end of a word.

Just like the letter D above, the ECI folks will unknowingly substitute the T sound, when it is placed at the beginning of a word, with the "ch" sound, turning "tube" into "choob" and "turnover" into "churnover."

Read the second sentence below. Then rewrite the sentence to how it phonetically should sound with an East Coast Irish accent. Here is an example.

The wee lad was done with his chores and ready for bed.

Te wee lahd was doon wit his chores and reedy fore behd.

Aye, the bonnie lass and her suitor were seen walking through the Irish glades this morning.

_____

_____

_____

_____

Voice - Part Two

Homework Assignment Eleven:

There is none! Keep working on your monologues and have your parent and/or guardian fill out the permission form, at the back of the book, for your observational field trip to a location where you can observe animal behavior. It could be a local zoo, lake or nature trail.

Application #9

Have you added enough inflection in your voice to keep your audience on the edge of their seats or do you still sound like a robot who is simply spitting out data that was saved by memorization? Were you brave enough to add an accent, if it was needed?

As uncomfortable as this might be, ask a family member or friend to watch you run through your monologue a few times. Ask for their input. Be willing to receive their criticism, even if you feel like it might be negative. A true actor must learn to take the lemons they receive and make lemonade. Otherwise they will never survive in the theatre.

Name _____ Relationship _____

On a scale of 1 to 5 (1 being strongly disagreed and 5 being strongly agreed), circle the scores that best summarize the student's performance. Please base your scores on their voice alone. How will you do this? Close your eyes, and listen.

Did I find the actor's voice engaging?
1   2   3   4   5

Did they sound like a monotone robot regurgitating their lines?
1   2   3   4   5

Did the actor make good use of dramatic pauses?
1   2   3   4   5

If they attempted an accent or dialect, did it work well within the context of the dialogue?
1   2   3   4   5

Additional Comments
_____
_____
_____

ACT ONE

Animals Can Be Inspirations Too

Lesson Thirteen

Animal Instincts

There is a reason that sentences like "meaner than a junkyard dog" and "wise as a barn owl" exist. Human beings can often possess the same innate and rather carnal characteristics of animals. You might be thinking, so what? How does that relate to acting? If your character is poised and full of grace, your inspiration might be a flamingo or a gazelle. If your character is grumpy and cantankerous, you might consider observing a bulldog or an opossum. Understanding the processes of animal behavior can have two main benefits for you, the actor. First, it is a fantastic way for you to develop a character, both physically and mentally, by really tapping into your imagination. Second, it allows you to experience instantaneous action and reaction to outside stimuli. Animals are driven by their base desires, just like humans. However, as an animal, you can really experience the "chase" of a want without over thinking the process. It is important to remember that, when you take on the characteristics of an animal, it is not an intellectual metamorphosis. Do not plan your actions or reactions. Trust that your honest observations of a certain animal have become fully assimilated into your memory so that when you eventually do become that animal, you will find its essence. Do not worry about how the shape of your body differs from that of the animal because you will be exploring its inner life and rhythms rather than simply representing its physical form.

Exercise One:
You are going on an observational field trip to either a local zoo, lake or nature trail. Please ask your parents to fill out the permission slip at the back of the book. Bring your Kitchen Sink workbook and a pen/pencil with you. Do not forget to bring money if there is an admission price, and money for a snack and/or drink. You will need to provide your own ride to and from the event.

ACT ONE

Choose four different animals (they can be mammals, reptilians, birds or any other creature at the location) that fascinate you. On the next three pages, observe and record their movements. Note how they interact with their environment and with their fellow animals. Think about what drives each animal; what it wants. Imagine yourself in its position and try to see the world through its eyes. What could be the corresponding human traits like grumpy, sneaky, paranoid, skittish, lazy, playful, etc.? Spend at least a half an hour at each location, do not just rush through this exercise. You will discuss your observations at the close of today's class.

Animal Number One

_____
_____
_____
_____
_____
_____
_____
_____
_____
_____
_____
_____
_____
_____
_____
_____
_____
_____
_____
_____

Animal Number Two

_____
_____
_____
_____
_____

Animal Instincts

Animal Number Three

ACT ONE

Animal Number Four

There will be no homework assignment this week. Just keep working on your observation skills and your monologue. See you next week!

Lesson Fourteen

Audition Tips

The big day has finally arrived. Auditions! Perhaps it is for a church drama team, a high school musical, a community play, a local film or admission to a well-known theatrical college. Despite the reason or venue, these auditions all share one common thread. No, it is not nerves or butterflies. It is preparation. You must be prepared for the audition that lies before you. But this begs the question, "How do I prepare?"

Some auditions will ask you to participate in a cold reading of their script with other actors. But most theatrical auditions will require a performance of two contrasting monologues (two to three minutes each): perhaps from different genres or periods of time. If you intend to seriously pursue acting in the future, now is the time to secure these monologues. Years ago, the place to find strong monologues was at the library or in a bookstore. Today, you have the world at your fingertips using the internet, so there is no excuse for not finding a suitable piece. It is important that you select monologues that will showcase your strengths and talents. Avoid pieces that contain a lot of cumbersome props (unless it is a small prop, like a cellphone or handkerchief). The idea of performing a monologue frightens some people because it is a solitary experience, alone in front of a panel of strangers. It can be very intimidating. To help you fully prepare your monologue, I suggest you concentrate on staging, pacing and proper eye line.

STAGING

Staging basically means figuring out where you will stand and how you will move in that space (aka. blocking). Construct a minimal set in your mind and utilize one chair or stool, if needed. Draw upon everything you have learned in Lesson Two through Lesson Six about sensory recall, and create a vivid setting with your imagination. When possible, sit down and write or draw the broader details of your character's world such as doors, windows, furniture

ACT ONE

or people. Include the small details of color and texture until you have recreated the entire environment. Then stand up and walk around your imaginary world, becoming familiar with that space. Be prepared to recreate that realm no matter where you physically are, whether it is in a church sanctuary in Springfield, Missouri or on a huge stage in New York City. If an actor can fully transport themselves into their character's world, they will feel safe and at home, forgetting about the critical eyes of the audition panel.

PACING

The fear of performing alone can sometimes prompt an actor to hurry through their lines in a terrified rush to their last spoken word. In that frenzied rush, they forget to use the stillness and pauses that help to bring their characters to life. Do not fall into that deadly trap. Allow these moments of stillness to occur, even if it feels like they might last a lifetime. Give your character a chance to think and feel before they speak their next line. This will lend an air of natural speech to your monologue, and therefore make the pacing seem more realistic. Above all, remain true to the fabric of your character and stay calm. Get your butterflies under control, or they will take control of your pacing, making you a nervous wreck. Immerse yourself in the character's environment, as described in the previous paragraph, and lean heavily on the relaxation techniques that were mentioned in Lesson Two, Relaxation, and Lesson Eleven, Voice Part One. Only then can you conquer your stage fright, and fully focus on the character inside that so desperately wants to get out.

EYE LINE

The quality of your "eye line" can either make or break your monologue. What does "eye line" even mean? It is the ability to place imaginary characters, costars in your scene, on the stage at the same time as you. And make them seem real. Are they sitting, standing or possibly moving? Your line of sight and subsequent reaction to these characters should convey to the audience where they are "physically" located in relation to you. Often inexperienced actors place their eye lines too low. For example, if an actor is speaking to an imaginary character who is seated on a chair, the actor will predictably look at the back of the chair, rather than a meter higher where the character's face would more likely be. Another common mistake occurs when a novice actor places an imaginary character beside them. When they do this, it forces them into a profile position (as discussed in Lesson Ten, Blocking) and thus, weakens the power of their performance. Remember to really "see" the character you are talking to on the stage. To convince yourself that you are speaking to someone else, try to visualize the other character so that they are actually present to you. The key is to make your audience believe that you are not alone. If you can accomplish that feat, then you are on the road to a successful audition.

Audition Tips

Exercise One:

Study the short monologue below. Mother and Stella are imaginary actors that you will interact with you in this monologue. Where will you place them in the scene? Is Mother seated or standing? Which side will Stella enter from, SL or SR? Play around with various placements. Everyone will be given ten minutes to memorize and block this short monologue. At the end of ten minutes, you will all be asked to present your interpretation to the class.

Stella has gone too far this time. She really has. And Mother, I know what you're thinking. You're thinking that this was all my fault. That I had this coming to me. Well, it's not my fault. It's not, I tell you. And I think it's high time that Stella be accountable for her crimes. (Stella enters) Ah, Stella! There you are. I've got something to tell you, young lady. You're not going to like it, but nevertheless, it must be said. Bad dog! You are a bad dog for chewing up my favorite pair of tennis shoes. It's the doghouse for you tonight! (Mother stands to leave) Mother, don't go. One night outside isn't going to kill her...

Did you happen to notice that Stella was a dog? Yes, a dog. It does not really matter if she were a human, a dog or even a chicken; she was a character who needed to be present in the sketch. We, the audience, needed to see her. How did you make her come alive? What could you have done differently? During monologues, treat these imaginary characters with the utmost respect. They might not be real, but if treated properly, they can be a major benefit to the success of your audition. And here are some more benefits, a list of Do's and Do Not's.

DO'S & DO NOT'S

Women

- Your hair should not be a distraction. Do not play with it or brush it out of your eyes, unless it is a part of the directions or a personality trait of your character. Your hair should be pulled up or pinned back from your face.

- Your makeup should be very light and natural.

- Avoid wearing a heavy perfume or body mist.

- If you must wear jewelry, keep it simple. Avoid earrings, necklaces or bracelets that sparkle or create jingling noises.

- Do not dress provocatively. You want the audition panel to look at your acting, not your chest or buttocks.

- Choose colors that will suit your complexion, and flee from clothing that has distracting logos or patterns on them.

- Never wear sweats or jogging pants.

- Wear comfortable shoes.

- Keep a bottle of water and a handful of cough drops nearby.

- Unless your character calls for it, your pockets should be off limits to idle hands. Your hands should be in full character mode, not buried in your clothing.

- Maintain an updated resume at all times.

- Secure some nice headshots.

Men

- Your hair should not be a distraction. Do not play with it or brush it out of your eyes, unless it is a part of the directions or a personality trait of your character. Your hair should be pulled up or pinned back from your face.

- Do not wear a hat since it will create a nasty shadow across your face.

- Avoid wearing a heavy cologne or deodorant.

- Choose colors that will suit your complexion, and flee from clothing that has distracting logos or patterns on them.

- Wear a belt. Nothing is more distracting than an actor pulling up their pants.

- Never wear sweats or jogging pants.

- Wear comfortable shoes.

- Keep a bottle of water and a handful of cough drops nearby.

- Unless your character calls for it, your pockets should be off limits to idle hands. Your hands should be in full character mode, not buried in your clothing.

- Maintain an updated resume at all times.

- Secure some nice headshots.

Audition Tips

Why are headshots so important? Headshots are one of the most effective tools an actor should possess to make a good, first impression on a producer or casting director. A headshot is a traditionally safe way of being able to decide an actor for a certain role based on the actor's natural look. Even an established actor needs to send their latest headshot photo along with an updated resume (sometimes the resume can be printed on the back of the 8x10). And speaking of resumes, I would be willing to bet that you have never drafted a resume before, right? That is okay. What better time to learn than now because if you wish to pursue a serious acting career or even audition for a local short film, you will eventually need a solid resume. Casting directors look at your resumes for your successes, where you are from, where you have been, what you have done, characters you have played, director and producers you have worked with, teachers you have had, where you went to school, etc. Everything is or should be, on your resume. It needs to contain your demographic information like name, date of birth, address, height, weight, hair color and eye color. In addition to your educational background, you will need to include a detailed list of all your past theatrical shows.

Homework Assignment Twelve:

Fill out the blank acting resume at the end of the book. Bring the completed form to your next class, which will mark the end of the Kitchen Sink Act One Workshop. You will perform your finished monologue at this class for your final grade. The proverbial drain has now been pulled; the water is all gone, and the soap bubbles have all disappeared. I sincerely hope your time at my sink has been profitable and a blessing to you. May God bless you in your future acting endeavors.

Application #10

Congratulations! You have reached the final application of The Kitchen Sink's Act One class. Sadly, it is not the time to celebrate just yet. It is, however, time to polish and apply the finishing touch to your monologue. As you run through it, be aware of your staging, pacing and eye line.

Step into the virtual setting of your monologue. Does it match the furniture that you have set before you on the stage? If there is a chair in your imaginary world, make sure there is a chair in the real world. Otherwise, you will attempt to sit and promptly fall. Draw a crude diagram of the staging you plan to use, including any chairs, benches, tables or doorways that you plan to use.

Have you added adequate pauses? Pay attention to how fast you deliver your lines. Are you delivering them too fast without giving your character time to formulate the sentences in their mind? Do not just spit your lines out like a robot. Deliver them with forethought and intention.

Are they any other characters within the context of your monologue?

Yes _____   No _____

Are you creating believable eye line heights for each one of them? Be careful not to make them appear like they are only one-foot-tall, especially if you have placed them in a sitting position.

ACT ONE
Dress Rehearsal Notes

ACT ONE
Sample Resume

Full Name

Phone Number

Email Address

Stage Experience

Show	Character	Theatre

Film Experience

Show	Character	Production Company

Training and Educational Background

Special Skills

ACT ONE
Character Sheet

Character Name _____ Estimated Age _____

Ethnicity: African American   Caucasian   Hispanic   Other

Socioeconomic Status: Wealthy   Middle Class   Poor   Unknown

Marital Status: Married   Divorced   Widowed   Single

Education: Elementary   High School   College   Doctorate

Personality Type: Introvert   Extrovert

Occupation (if applicable) _____

Brief Back Story _____
_____
_____
_____
_____

Goal or Objective
_____
_____
_____
_____
_____
_____
_____

ACT ONE
Character Sheet

Character Name _____ Estimated Age _____

Ethnicity: African American   Caucasian   Hispanic   Other

Socioeconomic Status: Wealthy   Middle Class   Poor   Unknown

Marital Status: Married   Divorced   Widowed   Single

Education: Elementary   High School   College   Doctorate

Personality Type: Introvert   Extrovert

Occupation (if applicable) _____

Brief Back Story _____
_____
_____
_____
_____

Goal or Objective
_____
_____
_____
_____
_____
_____
_____

ACT ONE
Character Sheet

Character Name _____ Estimated Age _____

Ethnicity: African American   Caucasian   Hispanic   Other

Socioeconomic Status: Wealthy   Middle Class   Poor   Unknown

Marital Status: Married   Divorced   Widowed   Single

Education: Elementary   High School   College   Doctorate

Personality Type: Introvert   Extrovert

Occupation (if applicable) _____

Brief Back Story _____
_____
_____
_____
_____

Goal or Objective
_____
_____
_____
_____
_____
_____

ACT ONE

Permission Forms

My child _____ has permission to meet her Kitchen Sink drama coach at _____ on _____/_____/_____. My cell number is _____ in case of emergency.

_____
_____/_____/_____
Signature   Date
I am available as a chaperone. Yes_____ No_____

My child _____ has permission to meet her Kitchen Sink drama coach at _____ on _____/_____/_____. My cell number is _____ in case of emergency.

_____
_____/_____/_____
Signature   Date
I am available as a chaperone. Yes_____ No_____

My child _____ has permission to meet her Kitchen Sink drama coach at _____ on _____/_____/_____. My cell number is _____ in case of emergency.

_____
_____/_____/_____
Signature   Date
I am available as a chaperone. Yes_____ No_____

My child _____ has permission to meet her Kitchen Sink drama coach at _____ on _____/_____/_____. My cell number is _____ in case of emergency.

_____
_____/_____/_____
Signature   Date
I am available as a chaperone. Yes_____ No_____

Notes

ACT ONE

www.ingramcontent.com/pod-product-compliance
Lightning Source LLC
Chambersburg PA
CBHW050455110426

42743CB00017B/3371